Slanguage
& GRIOT GLIMPSES
(Black Jesus Edition)
Poems 2002-2017

by
Slangston Hughes
(Victor F. Rodgers 2nd)

Copyright © 2017 Slangston Hughes
All rights reserved.

This book is dedicated to every poet who has ever inspired me, and even more importantly every poet who has ever befriended me, Thank You!

And also dedicated to Mary Jenkins, Devone Rodgers, Teresa Davis and Stacy Rodgers
The Cast Iron Roses who have nurtured sustained and kept me grounded throughout my entire life, Thank You!

Table of Contents

SLANGUAGE ARTS ... 7

- Slanguage Arts ... 8
- The Weight Within Words ... 12
- Street Poetry ... 14
- "Beneath The Surface " ... 16
- The Poetry of an Emcee ... 18
- Of Gods and Griots ... 20
- Spoken Scripture ... 23
- Cast Iron Roses ... 25
- Dedication… ... 27
- Pick Up The Pieces ... 31
- If seeing is believing, then show me the truth! ... 33
- The Devil's Cleansing ... 38
- H.A.A.R.P. Strings of the God's ... 41
- A Poem 4 The People ... 45
- Pray ... 47
- Crack Cake ... 49
- Mind Wine ... 52
- Deferred Dreams(Soliloquy of a Quiet Nightmare) ... 54
- A Dude Playing A Dude Pretending To Be Another Dude a.k.a.Obama-Nation(Part 1, The Post Modern Coup) ... 59
- Obama-Nation Part 2(Imperialism's True Face Revealed) ... 65
- Obama-Nation Part 3 ("the X's and O's of an enigma") ... 69
- "Theme 4 Inglish"(Da B-Mix) "I Gotta Write" ... 74

GRIOT GLIMPSES ... 79

- Return of the Griot ... 80
- Huey Freeman's Diary ... 82
- Free-dumb (Complacent Slavery) ... 85
- Yakub ... 89
- 91
- Why Does The Woolly Mammoth Howl At Midnight??? ... 92
- "Words Don't Die" ... 98
- X-Men ... 100
- SLANGSTON X ... 111

The Pedagogy Of Points 116
Sundiata Lives! 120

BLACK JESUS 130

Affirmation For Assata 131
The Flame 135
A Poor Man's Dream 139
True Blood 141
Kuumba 149
Alkebulan 154
Oshun's Revenge 157
Sagefo's Words 160
Sundiata Strikes Back 166
Ghetto Griot 173
Blood On My Pen 178
America On Fire 206

FOREWORD

Slangston Hughes is one of those poets that you can't believe that you actually met in person. He's the alien you've always heard about but didn't quite believe in, until now. Normally, someone like him is written about decades after you would have had the chance to see him perform.

Seeing him in action has always been a paranormal experience for me. During each performance, I have always been fully aware that I was witnessing what would one day be literary history. While he recites his poetry, I'm subconsciously crafting my own about the experience.

He has the rare ability to put into words what most people cannot craft into scattered thoughts. He is not only ahead of his times, he is behind them, channeling images and thoughts that the ancients would have shared if they had his tongue.

Chin-Yer Wright

Creator/Director of Word War Poetry Slam Series & "The Baltimore Scene"

Slanguage Arts & Griot Glimpses is both a chronicling of one individual's growth as a writer over a 15 year period of poetic evolution (2002-2017) - as well as a record of some of this era's most pressing sociopolitical issues and happenings as witnessed and responded to in arguably some of the most radical and profoundly truthful incantations ever written down via the medium of poetry in a manner where the political and personal merge. Slanguage Arts & Griot Glimpses is very much "A research guide for the soul."

SLANGUAGE ARTS

Slanguage Arts

Awaking from a Deferred Dream
I hear the spirit of Langston Hughes
spitting stanzas over Weary Blues

So forget red ink and corrections
the street essence holds the blessing

The people speak through me
and their dialect is my message

Yo son I play on words like kids on asphalt
overtime poetic lines collect poetic bruises
this is musical revolt

So "check check check check check check
check out my melody"
killed so many mics I got 9 innings worth of strikes
and they all felonies

Hey yo hey yo hey yo
peep these mathematics

Truth divided by lies carry the solution
from hear back to Jerusalem
yet the seed of Ephraim still possess negative solutions polluted by madness

youknowhatimean

Write like my pen slice that uncut
leave it stuck

In each stanza

so what up dunn taste some
poetry so dope it keep my tongue numb
like agggghhhhhhsghaaaaaaaaaaahahjejahhhhhh

As you can see this is not necessarily for your bookshelf

Spell-check would go crazy trying to run through my text

All traditional rules of grammar get left suspended

Like students in need of discipline

Now watch me flip it like contradictions

It is what it is
don't like it shouldn't have brought us

So if you young rich and white
scared of getting robbed at night
it ain't my fault
you inherited these problems when yo ancestors bought us

You can't ignore the hood son
the ghettos the foundation
don't believe me just check your vertebrae for footprints
cause the have knots be like gravity
holding everybody else down

Well actually up cause they all standing on us
while we collect no ends plus determine the trends
like Richard Pryor telling the citizens of the Emerald City what the color of the day is

Why you think they lie in the sun trying to get shaded?

everybody talking about bling bling and for shizzle my nizzle
but as soon as a real nizzle run up like
run that bling bling or this gun going sing sing
and splinizzle your wizzle
all of a sudden you want to give me my grammar back

In exchange for the shirt off my back

Well F.uck U B.ack U.p
burry you on a Hill and I don't Figure that Tommy
is hardly able to relate
and the same goes for Uncle Tom Sean
sitting on the Jean shitting out wack records

My great great great great grandmother
boiled Phat on the Pharm just to feed the family

Cause I'm from the ghetto where souls get left frozen
cause they come colder
than the South Pole in the middle of October

So don't get mad
when I switch the ingredients in your recipe

It's easy

Cause I'm used to making Kool-Aid
out of dry lemons and melted popsicles

don't believe me?

Shit just give me some old oranges and lime flavored freezes
and see exactly what I'm capable of

We soul survivors
thrive off of whatever we got
this is not sonnets and Shakespeare
some people call it Street Poetry
cause my page contains the block

And I stand on corners spitting out jewels
like a rapper from the dirty south
who just got punched in the mouth
with a fist made of bricks

Bite off a little bit

Speech is concrete

My lyrical content sits like broke Volvos on spinners
cause even when the money stop my mind keeps spinning
so I'm winning
with designs from thee who holds a higher position
the most high develops the fire I'm spitting
so forget ice I just stand in front of this mic
receive light in my life and instantly glisten

Please pay close attention to the mission
my aims much different
and it's clearly the truth that their missing
and without it they poetry resembles legless kickers
trying to hit field goals
and that shit just ain't getting it

Rappers forget your jewels, cash and whip
your tongue, lungs, saliva and diction
nigga run that shit
cause you're whack and shouldn't be spitting

And this is authentic
not literary fiction
just the experience
I'll prepare you much better than merely
the lone limits of simplistic academics

I inserted truth into the mic so that what I write could stand apart
Created a blueprint for my own language what I give you is
Slanguage Arts

Awaking from a Deferred Dream
I hear the spirit of Langston Hughes

spitting stanzas over Weary Blues

So forget red ink and corrections
the street essence holds the blessing

The people speak through me
and their dialect is my message

The Weight Within Words

Ever since God spit that first phrase, "let there be light"
the word has existed and coexisted with the world
for that word has been life, clutching to mics we might attempt to recite the meaning
searching our entire lives for what has always been
so through this search artistically fire gets put into pens
released like flamed speech through a verse, bars go past the margins and don't stop at the end, from lack of poetic patience
scribbled maps on kitchen tables
trying to find a destination that makes $ense
cause somewhere along the way money became the foundation of what we believe to exist
so civilizations were constructed with carnivorous cement
while preachers pimp salvation like a ho named music
and Klan's men yell repent, the word ceases to be truth if we choose to miss use it
that's why I want just the thought out concoctions of each thought that I'm dropping
to make merciless minds shiver, when divine designs are delivered
for certain you worthless merchants will have to remember
as I put the weight on you like Samson ripping down two pillars
more than just a simple spitter verbal killer
vicious flame emitter making souls quiver
never enough, heavy concentrations of vocal indentations
I construct are clearly to real to touch, on impact
your reactions will never be able to adjust
to the point that the only response that comes up is WHAT?

therefore I breathe these intense lyrical degrees with relative ease
for it is the prophet who foresees and attempts to redeem
for he knows that one day very soon
even that invincible king shall also fall to his knees
in essence where just pawns put into play on the board
by opposing players
and the pieces in which they compete for our are souls
now watch close as Satan attempts to take hold
maneuvering his rook into position in order to
deviate attention from the knight's schemes
to capture the lives of ghetto queens, as death and hatred impose their will through evol influence, but if you can see what's
truest in the end it's ourselves that we kill
puzzling while the pieces on the board maneuver
in ignorance ignoring the lord
and fire loaded pieces in war, as Lucifer laughs while more pointless pints of blood are poured, in these last days where it
seems angels cease to sing
but fear not, because the Elohim is still true king

checkmate on your memory
forgotten history
distorted imagery
steering through cracked mirrors we see the true enemy
sharp edges cut deeply, racing through desperate destinations
I'm tracing this with a giant chisel into big sheets of concrete
because just paper can't possible hold the weight

of this piece
the massive clashes of wars raged stay in caged in each bar
these contents are chilling, in between each breath exists the unheard screams and scattered words of motherless children,
the weight within these words recorded the sounds of mass killings, the reason caskets keep filling
voices who inspire choices that invoke the hands of fate to squeeze communities till they choke, looking for solutions to the mental pollution damaging most
phases of parable phrases caught in my throat
indeed I proceed with quotes, exhale these spiritual spells like weed smoke

I write poems dedicated to the hated and trife
poems dedicated to death that serve as reflections of life
and if I didn't spit, the weight within these words would stay trapped inside my lungs
and probably crush my windpipe
mouth to mic resuscitation, I'm trying with all my might to revive the crowd tonight
giving through my hearts beat patterns prolific poly-rhythms
sparking the torment from forgotten years
my tremendous text left lyrics printed into the trail of tears
lost prophet with no profits and a fuzzy identity
I'm a fucking mutt, got African, German, Israeli, Portuguese Blackfoot, Seminole and Cherokee all wrapped up in me driven by infinity
cause the voices of my ancestors demand that I remember me

you want to get to know the poet who be flowing like a raging river
so in retrospect I always lose focus but then meet up with myself again
when thoughts speak through pens at a particular point in space and time
where the remaining remnants of existence stop spinning
and eventually the beginning greets the end

you can feel the massive amounts crashing down on your soul's reserves
observe and yes be highly concerned
as you bare witness when I'm spitting
to the weight within words

Street Poetry

Yo this is street poetry
Incantations for the pavement
They call it street poetry
But only God could save them

And yea I hear you speaking but what do your words equal
where's the purpose lie?
have you analyzed the mission of your compositions?
who's your diction dedicated to?

me, I'm kind of like Common on the corner
or Langston in Harlem
I write for the people
and the pavements my sequel
attached to my pallet remains the most potent dosage
and I keep wet ink on the bottom of my footwear
so that the words I write walk with me
carve my cadence in concrete and carry it
a true street poet

catch me at the intersection of life and death
nearly out of breath
trying to find the balance between cursed and blessed
but who knew they were twins
who wrestled in the womb
and had nightmares about Leviathan
my lyrical content is higher than underground
looked inside my soul and found the sound of heaven

"and there's so much on my mind
that I don't want to recline"
shooting holes in the fake flesh of Christ
until I saw the true son of God begin to shine
because sometimes
Satan I'll knock on your door
wearing a homemade Jesus mask
just so he can get inside
loot your salvation and fuck your spirit in the ass
and it's around this point that I begin to ask
what on earth am I writing?

walking from the subway with my pen out notebook in hand
etching and sketching connections
of confused chicken scratch on to this pad
I'm restless, barely watching where I'm stepping
almost got hit by a car and shit
hanging on to half of a word tripping over the curve
mix sawdust with cement plus 27 liters of my spit
forget what you heard

this is Street Poetry
incantations for the pavement
so like famous white figures attending Klan rallies
I keep the hood close to me

"and there's so much on my mind
that I'd die if I tried to recline"
shooting holes in my own soul
trying to find peace on these lines

and I can feel the city breathing
but she's bleeding at the same time

her inner demons got her leaning like towers in Pisa
and I'm supposed to be believing
subways shoot like needles
through tunnels that are her veins
and heroin remains the last train leaving
and I can hear Nina Simone singing like

"Oh Baltimore"

because I speak for the people and the streets speak to me
my pen bleeds these paragraphs I just plead on their behalf
so please lend your ears and listen to the pavement

This is street poetry
Incantations for the pavement
They call it street poetry
But only God can save them

"Beneath The Surface "

Turn off your radio
Throw away your adidas sneakers
Dispose of your spray cans
And burn all yours cd's cassettes and classic vinyl
MC's must have missed the memo
Because apparently it seems HipHop is dead
That's right dead

Lifeless, extinct, no longer matters
Or at least that's what my ears pick up when I stop
to observe all the chit chatter
As the spit gathers in my throat
Everybody's got they own "Low End Theory"
On why HipHop is no longer breathing
but I refuse to believe it
Cause there's too much Evidence
that clearly disproves their thesis

It is ridiculous
how an individual can claim
to fully for see the truth
When their perception remains limited
Yet somehow cynics and critics remain so inconsistent
And claim that HipHop is no longer living
When it's only a small portion of the music to which that they're actually listening

Only view and place analysis on the small percentage
of the cultures existence that they're witnessing
then possess the audacity to actually place judgment on this sacred expression as a whole

It is impossible to come to a full over-standing of anything
before first analyzing all available angles, perspectives, data and elements

And speaking of elements I really wish
these ignorant ass ma fuckers would stop condemning
all of HipHop for the so called sins of one refinition

Now pay attention

To these things that clearly need to be mentioned
this is for all the ill graph writers and dope spitters
it's time for the awakening dedicating this
to all turntablists, forgotten beatboxers and b-boys
who never stopped innovating true HipHop elevation

This is more than just music don't act stupid
and confuse it with merely the mic
these close minded idiots got me losing patience

because HipHop is life yet still
so many people choose to waste it
and refuse to put their ears to the pavement and listen to the underground

Dig deep "Beneath The Surface"
where the true jewels are found
and the third golden era of HipHop music
is clearly alive and breathing vibrantly

So follow me, follow me into a world of Eyedea's and Abilities where dope Doctors of Doom
practice Madvillainy
and Little Brother's
raised off of a truer era evoke the masses to start listening

Again
to real rhymes and dope beats
from Killah Priest
who practice Jedi Mind Tricks
with an Immortal Technique
yes it gets deep, yes it gets deep

But to me it's clear that HipHop still lives
somewhere in the Atmosphere where Aesop Rocks
and De La drops on "The Grind Date"
so I bump beats from "My Own Worst Enemy"
by Ed O.G. and Pete Rock to keep my mind straight

cause now days Nikki Minaj gets more play
than Mc Lyte or Jean Grae
so I turn up a little J Live or Foreign Exchange
while smoking on some Canibus in the mist of all the K-os
in order to maintain
cause money long since replaced what matters most in music
and the "Damage" is "Fantastic"
so most so called cultural purist
don't even want to cop El-P's (LP's)

Cause the true meaning, well "The True Meaning"
seems to have been tarnished and "The Realness" in HipHop is hard to manage

But please if nothing else over-stand this
and actually put your ears to the surface
and listen to the resistance
where lyricist still spit that real shit

The Poetry of an Emcee

Hold tight with a death grip on the mic like my life depended on it
This is my form of the blues slang is what I choose
And use Ebonics to paint pictures through the tune
You can hear the fierce unspeakable languages of fate in the wind
Lost for years but finally through ink and tears we translate again
And transmit through mics the regained truths squeezed out of pens with rage
Mentally deranged my thoughts like runaway slaves
So I freestyle on the page land on stage and recite flames
Poetically musical trains of thought fail to escape in the night causing mental pain
My heart pumps an endless rhythm tracks stuck in my veins
So I can't stop spitting, off the top of the brain I remain addicted
Ripping contenders to shreds like unwanted written compositions
Devour and digest lyricist, let the world be my personal commode
As I defecate on competition with a vicious strike
Despicable type, sprinkle fecal matter on mics
This is the way I release, lost spirits exist in my speech
Eternal life through scriptures I write ignites fires in the street
My pen reflects history on text, reflections of what's next
Trying to collect what's left, through drifting minutes push this expression to the limit
I spill these poems endless, digging in the dark for what once was
Constant war battle myself in the basement scribbling verses on old cardboard
Forbidden thoughts strangled by mic-chords
It began on that cold December day when I stepped upon a small wooden stage
Mind completely on blank, steering at the crowd with shit to say
Tongue touched by God and suddenly words just came
First lyrics to ever sprout out my mouth
I was cursed with the blessing of poetic speech
Stressing at night I see visions of verbal collisions in my sleep
Messages sent from the ancients in flow form
Moving across the waters landing in strange places
Griping to my pen trapped in concealed spaces
Looking at known unfamiliar faces
My dreams relate to life in a way most hated and trife
Trying to make sense of this senseless strife
I strike pages with an uncontrolled intensity in the night
Burn phases of parable phrases on bricks, the knowledge is non-essentially thick
Sinking in memories flashbacks attack relentlessly
From the past of a future that's already occurred visually
My poetry's pure reality, causalities reflected traced out through tragedies
Like Shakespeare at his desk holding a tech
To live or not to live? Is the question contemplated prior to death?
Ravage retarded ratings of a mad man written in rhyme
Testified on stage like revelations, rugged revered holding weapons
Pacing, ready to stick up the congregation, collect the plates and change location
Racing through life on the pages lines, always two steps behind
Enslaved by each line, placed in shackles by my own intuition
Distorted position from what was written, steady slipping
Writing utensils grip-less, no identity like my finger prints were missing
They tried to hide my linage by rearranging dates
Erasing sacred strides stroked into the sands of time
While tampering with the scribes from inside the makers mind
Seeking even deeper to see what I find
Nothing but
Old crushed up microphones, broken pencils, ink-less pens and shredded rhymes
Emotional archeologist, dug deep into my brain and came up with this

I'm sorry to say it ya'll, but we ain't shit
A soulless spec in the massive universe of confined verses
Slowly dying at rapid rates, whose speeds increase due to the curses
Quietly placed in between each carefully squeezed piece of unheard speech
Worthless bars bounce back to me off the walls of my brain cells
The pain excels at rates even greater insane creator
What I give you write here, is a brain aneurysm placed on paper
Simultaneous spontaneous combustion of ravenous thoughts rushing
Over cardiac percussion attacking your lack for useful function
Soul seeker write with the sight of the reaper
ghosts who gargle with liquid verses might greet ya
scream and blow out weak stereo speakers with poison poetic procedures
Sure *I use to love her* but *common sense* tells me I should leave her
The poetry of an emcee hold my pen like a heater, BLAH!

Of Gods and Griots

If you choose not to refer to me as poet or emcee
then simply acknowledge me as Jedi
carry the stories of the people beneath my tongue
my spoken poetry holds words
much heavier in worth and weight
than the remixed textbooks of historical fiction authors
my diction offers simply the truth

These speech patterns echoed generations
far before fake gangstas set foot in a booth
so as soon as Mr. Hughes starts spitting you witness
the continued existence of oral tradition
and my ears are therefore immune
to the confused mission and position
of so called scholarly representatives
who snooze inside the pages of their prisons
I mean, anthologies
And sleep on this
Vocal verbally vintage ancient holy spoken scripture
and if they'd awake for one second they'd see
that they were much more than simply resting
but actually dependent on this foundation
once laid like pyramids in the dessert
you cannot fully translate my hieroglyphics
so you instead underestimate their worth
question their purpose
and have doubts about this power

However in the final hour
when pens have been long since silenced
and manuscripts of questionable text set to flame
my words shall remain like a haunting voice in the night
somewhere in Ghana or London
Tokyo, Panama, Afghanistan or Baltimore
decayed ears and reincarnated souls shall come back to life
rise from the minds of murdered children
just to hear the griot recite
and tell the story that written rhetoric disguised with lies
squeezed in between 2 truths and biblical text
with missing chapters was too one sided to tell
these are tales you cannot tell
on recycled trees and cd's

So what's really the reason for this infinite
conflict of interest?
between the oral and written traditions
I mean if it is by the hand of God that truth is written
than what's the difference whether poetry is read or spitten?
because I have this on paper does it make it any less true?
and if I simply print it submit it commit it and spit it
does that take away from the meaning of its existence?
in the beginning was the word
God spoke and it became flesh
He didn't first refer to an excerpt from the text
and if She did would that quote once spoke be therefore any less blessed?

Now let's take some time to address this entire concept of "Bless The Mic"
you see I truly believe that the modern day griot
slash spoken word artist
slash poet
slash emcee
when practicing their craft properly is about as close to G.o.d.
as any human being in the physical form can possibly be
and if these poetic verses aren't properly serving their purpose as prophesy
then our full potential as poets has not been reached
who have we touched and who have we reached
perhaps the same couple freaks who frequent the venue each week
so poets pen surpluses of pornographic poetic orgies
on page
and no I'm not knocking your oratory orgasmic game
but too much of anything can be bad for you
including sex pieces
so watch out for these poetic plagues
cause some of these artist be dirty and like to spread
spoken aids
clearly everything's not what it seems to be these days
all I'm trying to say is that a sense of
balance needs to be obtained
they say life is made up of both yin and yang
positive and negative
placed on both sides of these poetic fences
so when it comes to this division
between oral and written tradition
despite the blurry lines and confused minds
who try to categorize their difference
clearly more can be obtained
"if we just strain"
and take some time to see
how much both are equal integral parts of each other's existence

so why should E The Poet Emcee or Taalam Acey
be seen as having any less literary credibility
than your poets who push books or rock pages off of podiums
and this doesn't necessarily mean that
Cornelius Eady
Linda Joy Burke
or Men Maa Aim Ra
aren't just as lyrically nice with what they write and recite
than those who some consider as your illest slam poets and spoken word artists
honestly enough with the labels already
did Ginsberg, Kerouac and Ferlinghetti
not pave the way for today's performance poets with published books in hand the whole way
truth be told it's all about what you say when you speak
cause I then seen both Baraka and Madhubuti blaze the stage
with just as much intensity as your illest slam champion
and never even leave their seat
in actuality it all comes from the same source
the creator just gives us the permission to spit it out

so if Gods could really converse with Griots
what do you think they would talk about?

Spoken Scripture

A very Komplex writer once said that
"these poets are not prophets"
and these
"poems are not prophecy"
truth spoken, unfortunately

however if this is indeed "God's Work"
then believe me they need to be
in order for us as both artists and human beings
to reach our full poetic potential
both lyrically and spiritually
I don't think ya'll hear me
Listen...

As far as my styles considered the "E" in Torchlight clearly represents more than simply entertainment
Let's raise the level and Evolve into elevation
carve my poetry in graffiti on Pyramids and have Ra E-Mix it with angel's vocals
you see I spit spoken spirit in seven different frequencies
until even demons get their ears scorched
I don't preach to choirs I speak with fire
and engulf fake saints with this mic stand that I make morph into a torch
light it ignite it recite it when I'm finished start inviting these shit talkers to the stage
baptize them in blood and flames
you see I came to cleanse souls like colons
so hear these finger prints that I form into poems
and leave scattered across brains
let each thought take control
they say that God spoke and the word became flesh
so I guess that without a spirit flesh is just dead dust
so words must have a soul
and I got the ghost of ghetto griots living in my pages
spitting and exchanging inspiration for patience
cause they waiting
for a poet dope enough to simply speak
and bring phrases, pages, pictures plus scriptures into instant existence
so that when I start spitting the spirits of slain slaves and street soldiers
are set free through saliva and pain
merged with pure soul I give you this perfect mixture
far beyond merely words these poems are spoken scripture

for instance
"and the lord delivered unto to me two notebooks of stone
Written with the finger of God"
and on them was written the illest poem of all time
spawned from divine design
and my pen is simply an extension of Him or hymns
I'm not really writing more like drafting a message
crafting a blessing
yet "the words of his mouth were smoother than butter
but war was in his heart
so my soul is among lions
and I lie even among them
that are set on fire
even the sons of men whose teeth are spears and arrows
and their tongue a sharp sword"
poets be careful whose mouth's you turn your back towards
sure some of these writers spit fire but nothing their tongue ever touches gets cleansed
"ye ye stand upon your sword, ye work abomination defile your neighbor's wife"
deep concentration my creation encompasses the mic
"and the word of the lord
came unto me saying
son of man prophesy against the Shepherd's"
who deceive the people like lost sheep lyrically leading them to the slaughter
an angel gave me a kiss and spit a poem inside my mouth
so if I was to juice my tongue out it would probably produce holy water
"see the light of the body is the eye, therefore when thy eye is single
thy whole body is also filled with light
but when thine eye is evil, the body also is full of darkness"
so I stick my pen inside the minds of wicked men
spark flames of purity
and poetically light torches of truth
"and I saw in the write hand of him that sat on the throne
a book written within
and on the back side sealed with seven seals"
so you see it is clearly my responsibility as
his or her mouth piece
to present these poems as prophecy
or otherwise I'd obviously be falling short of my destiny
so over-stand that what you have witnessed
is far more than simply poetry
this is Spoken Scripture

May God add a blessing to the spitting of this word

Cast Iron Roses

2-Pac once said that we should "thank God and celebrate the tenacity of the roses that manage to grow from concrete"

well I'm here to tell you that my roses
were just a bit more than simply tenacious
they were amazing
a status far above those weltering buds
that simply blow away when the winds get harsh
you could strike cold winds like metal to their hearts and indeed receive a spark
igniting true life and love
these were more than your usual gentle peddles that the world likes to ignore
and leave trampled by the wayside of time
legacy lost and frozen

I'm talking about Cast Iron Roses
known for upholding the truth
provided me with steel roots all throughout my youth
so when thorns and thickets tried to get in the middle
I was able to stay grounded
due to their guidance and nourishment
so now I'm serving this like home cooked meals
with a pinch of mama magic
stories get mixed with something tragic
in the ghetto residents where life gets packed with madness
and adolescents sale packs of momentary gladness
that routinely morphs into lifelong addiction and sadness
you see regular roses bloom in good weather
and when the season is right
sure that's easy
however cast iron roses not only survive
but find ways to thrive through hard winters
cast iron like them pots
that hang in grandma's kitchen
I'm talking cast iron like that Franklin wood burning stove
in the living room
better feed the fire
got to cut the kindling keep the kids warm
but yet always still manage to bloom in full beauty like that rose-bush in the front yard

You see, life's trials make us who we are
the creator designs are nature
fully equips us for what we need in order to survive the storm
I'm talking cast iron roses that pack thick thorns
my mother ripped a switch from those roses
and tore my tale up
that time I tried to throw my sister
from the top of
the staircase

thorns and all

this beautiful bouquet is clearly a rare case
I'm talking cast iron roses with names like
Mary, Paulette, Devone and Teresa

strong enough to hold a house hold up
when the winds blew they never wavered
just worked with what was given
at times trampled and nearly smothered beneath
pieces of hardship tragedy and broken concrete
but still stood their ground regardless
cast iron roses with "patches" on their souls
cast iron roses like Maggie Hearing and Sarah Davis
more than tenacious amazing
I'm talking Stacy, Shelly, Mamme, Iris, Ernestine,
Justine and Sarah Weaver
weave these poetic procedures like fine fabric deep
into your souls tapestry
some might call it resilience, I refer to it as mastery
cause I was raised by strong women who mastered
the
art of living
for they say nothing is ever too much to deal with
when compared to the amount that God giveth
these are my bloodlines observe how I spit them.

You see, you made me me
so I rep for warriors who wear scars like medals
sprouted steel peddles like wings
and more than just wiggled their way through the cracks
but truly penetrated solid pavement
and broke their way through
"cast iron roses" this is for you black woman
while they constantly continue to call you out of your name
but you see a Rose is still a Rose and for me your worth
has always remained

for my Cast Iron Roses

Dedication...

It was love at first write

connected with her thoughts like eye contact

her pupils were pages

steered onto the lines and into her mind, and oh was it so beautiful

infatuated with her stories, from pain that gave way to elegant phrases

the world tried to strip her of dignity and grace

leaving her spiritually naked

so she clothed her soul in metaphors and pages

poetry was her everything

you can hear HipHop in her talk with rhythm in her walk

left footprints like sonnets as her-story

where she stood was the present

steps visualized on her path

scripted out poetically in paragraphs gave us hope for the future

so she drew poetry like self-portraits in diaries and

personal journals

you see men had forgot her worth

so she used words to redefine it

rather screaming out on stages or keeping creativity concealed to closets and notebooks nonetheless that paper

was her savior

yes her pen went deep and this queens beauty was beyond skin deep

she sported scars that were gorges, really couldn't control my reaction

cause her wounds simply proved her worth and experience

the imperfections made her perfect

so each so called flaw made her appear even more attractive

I mean her skin is made from three layers of poetic verses

symphony's play whenever she speaks

and every time that she bleeds the world drinks from her ink

so she keeps turning pages and flipping phrases

as she goes through various stages of living

baptize myself in her saliva gaining divine inspiration every time she starts spitting

she's my goddess and my griot, heroine to so many

sister, daughter, mother, cousin, student, full time employee, your cool auntie, poet, songstress, extra dope lyricist, my favorite femcee,

so many often fail to remind her of her worth

so she hides the hurt deep inside a verse

but ain't it funny how God works

because all of her pain just happened to be the source of her beauty

no poetry I could ever write I'll be able to fully capture the essence of thee

a blessing indeed

took the trials and tribulations of life

and made a dope style throwing inspiration all over my "blank pages" when she writes....

I dedicate this to all my oh so lovely lady lyricist

I imagine the perfect kiss still wouldn't be equivalent to the poems you spit

"this is dedicated to, this is dedicated to, no this is dedicated to,"

the poetress who writes priceless

bringing forth *Lyfe* as she recites with insight from her

3rd Eyesis

this is dedicated to "spoken soul" artists with thick *Hips* who rep for *Ja* and Aphrodite live on the grind in the *B*

but stay *Fly*

C Clear through the madness, and to spite the *Mzery*

still write they own book of rhymes and call it "Herstory"

giving out "Moments Vocally" like *V Poetess* with the bravery of well

Brave, Veronica, Amanda Fair, HanaLyn, Joanna Hoffman and yes *Ms. Stress*

when she sings I swear I can hear "Meditative Soul" fill the air like *Chin-Yer*

yo this is house music like *Jeneba Suma*

too many tried to miss use ya, so she reveals *Da Truth* in each line

while sipping on some *Green Tea* with a little *Honey* inside her *Green Eyes* she sighs and begins artistically

creating a Synergy out of *Rah Energy* you can *C Love* on her mind while supplying mo fire than *Gaia*

and breaking it all the way down to the *Symantyx* when she rhymes

in her prime every piece is created equally like all *Tayree's*

this is dedicated to *Lady's* who drop *Wisdom* within

Deferred Dreams

and scream out frequencies of pure reality in their poetry until all nightmares cease

we often fail to see how life can be so *Unique*

in the streets were beasts make attempts at *Robin-sons* of their existence

this is for all my sisters too nervous to share their verses but I guarantee if you simply dig deep enough into your *Vision*

you'll find roots to *Urban Flowers* plus a *Jewel* similar to *Black Diamonds*

hiding beneath the surface

and it's true because of you I now write with a new *Purpose*

I'd be ten times the lyricist if just an inch of you'll spirit was to embrace my page

as pens stroke hearts her *Love-Laces* the lines of fate

metaphors like malaises hitting your plate possessing poetic content so thick

she could use just her words and build a House of Bricks like *Sonya Renee*

or like *Notre*, *Princess Bunny* and *Lady J* cause you know they stay with a familiar face and hold up, let me make

sure I properly pronounce the name *Adar Ayira*

yea ya'll I hear ya

cause this is for every *Rebecca Dupas, Constance, Missy, Tyresa, Sharde* and *Emonefala* cause *She Rock's* with

timing like a Dj

or like *Naima J*

spitting fire as if she was snacking on kerosene and matches until the mics wires expire from metaphoric

magnetic attraction interacting with da page like yeah.

With intricate text flowing through sets you can see her *Lyric-in-spect*.

Hold up, *Jackie Terry*. What more do I even need to say?

not to mention *Rhonda L.T.* plus shit talking shorties like *Tera* and *Tanye*

Whitney you C it be like an *Anomaly*

cause honestly her similes be continually shining like the sun

providing me with *Soul-R-Inner-g*

and even if there's *Rayne* in the *Autumn*

at those times when life seems deeper than *Pockets*

you can still receive a little *Nappy Logic*

from *Black Butterflies* and *Queens*

who converse beside *Angels*

who scribble scribes with ink that's *Golden* and pen *Infamous* lines

hope ya'll never stop writing….

and at night it's like I seen *McKenna* in the *Moon*

dedicated to the Muse of Slangston Hughes

I need ya

so keep singing like *Kelita*

cause this be for *Butterfly's* who claim "Revenge" in the name of "Dandelions"

as well as *Queens* of distant lands like *Sheba*

I'm penning this in the name of H.E.R.

no not HipHop but when my heart beat drops

she speaks so *Unique* with poetry that's *Heaven Sent*

and even if holy lyrical *Trilogies* cease to exist

when she writes, even in times of so called *Silence*

there's always *Love* inside the lines so you just can't help but *S.m.i.l.e.* all the time

and you know that I'm write

shit, before it's all said and done God knows I'm probably going make a poet my wife

synchronize my heart beat with her heart beat like

1, 2,

I dedicate this

to you……………..

Pick Up The Pieces

Scatter my thoughts over these pages like shattered promises throughout the ages
speak with a tongue so broken that they call these poems tasteless
continually caught in the mix, of so much bullshit
that from a cultural perspective my roots are nearly traceless
snapped off at the stem the lack of nourishment stems
from crack vials and shots of gin, while shots fire and the murder rate rises again
you can't erase this I wrote it from within
spawned by pressure that's intense spoke it and birthed a gem
in dreams bullets pierce my skin
leaving jewel shards scattered across pages and bloody pavement
so now I'm desperately reaching seeking speaking with pieces attached to my being
Slangston Hughes crack open a wound
and see how I spill this ill street speech until it fills the room
let the real sneak through cracks in the concrete where crack addicts sleep
I wish my words could make motionless men move
and prove that these fraudulent fallacies are not true
they simply assume us doomed due to the fact that the ghetto is where we grew
on blocks were brothers feud
sipping life's liquors from pitchers of sadness
and eating generic fruit loops with blacked spoons
we receive 4th and 5th best from food banks and hell fare checks
it's like share cropping for the new century
mention me and seek me out on missions be seeking for identity in spiritual cemeteries bury poems like obituaries

we write pieces
somebody pick em up
we recite pieces, did anybody pick em up
you know what
fuck these pieces, we need to pick them up
enough
forget developing from exposed positives and negatives
take these pieces and put pictures of the truth together
so if consciousness is what you claim to be peddling let's settle it
stop talking and do something, prove something
stop standing in place and let's collectively move something
poets claim to spit flames in the name of respect clutching to empty decks
mother fucker stop bluffing, its nothing, fake revolutionaries fronting
so called televised Gil Scott Heron remakes lack
the substance of the original
biting criminals
word to Native Son
I'm about to snatch my tongue out
and tag you with it on Facebook
just so I could say I spit, delicate digitals to an audience of hypocrite individuals
it's really simple though, listen yo, my dictions broke, my dictions broke
like I cued up alphabet cereal and tried to spit a poem
"the words won't fit in my mouth"

but see, I Care-More like Jessica, listen Black I'm Pressing ya
got the hands of the lord on me like son don't you feel it
I'm testing ya
cause if you don't do for you and yours than nobody else will
this is not poetry, this shit is for real
and when it comes to Inglish, I break like Ken Swift
on cardboard
Mr. Glass
politician's promises and treaties with Native Americans
my language stays shattered like black communities and the hearts of mourning mothers while the projects be like Towers of
Babel
a whole lot of niggas talking
but we obviously fail to understand one another
so in the words of Pete Rock
"Listen, just listen" except I'm not reminiscing
my dialect is broken like the Bible, way too many missing scriptures
broken like a smokers lung after too many years of use and vocal abuse
Slangston Hughes is not a myth my notebook is the proof
so I spit these rhyme schemes like shattered dreams
trying to awake slumbering minds to the truth
cause when it comes to this Slanguage
I break it down like

⚹♍♌●□⌑⚹♍ □□□⚹●♍□⚹♍ □♍☊● ■♍☊& ⚹♍□◆♓⚹ ♍□☊♍& ♌● ■⚹♍
♍□■♍□♍⚐ ⚹♍□♍ ♍□☊♍& ☊♎♎♌□□ ●♍♍• ♌♌⚹ O♑ □□□♎ ♍□◆●⚐
O☊&♍•••■☊O♍☊☊♍ •♍⚹∺⌧ •□ ■⚑•

⚹◆□■□♍O☊□O♌♌□□⚹□•♌□•⚹⚹♌♍ •⚹⚹∺♍⚹ •⊗
•◆■♓ ☊⚹□♍ □☊♑ □ O☊■♑♑♍☊□ □⚹ ◆□ ☊♎ ❖□☊• ☊♐◆♍
••☊■♓□□■ ✍◆♓⚹♍ ♌♌ ■□ O♑⚹ O♑ ■□♍♑♌□& ♌♌ ⚹♍ •□□∺• □□ ☊
♍□••♑□☊♍♎ ♌♌⚹ ⚹♍ •⚐⌚□⚑•♌♌ ⚹♍♍ □♑O♍ ♍⚹♍O♍
•♌♌&♍ ⚹☊☊♍□♍♎ ♎□☊O□ □□♌♌■♓ □□ ☊☊&♍ □•◆♓♍□♌♌■♓
O♌♌■♏ □□ ⚹♍ □□◆⚹• ♍☊◆♍ ⚹♍■ ♌♌ ♍□O♍ □□ ⚹♌♌
••☊♓◆☊♓♍• □ ♐□☊&♍ ♌♌ ♎□■ •♌♌&♍

Yet it all still remains hopeless
so I ripped off both my ears with a Van Gogh type of focus
so that maybe I'll actually be considered a Def Poet
but then again I'd probably get censored like Amiri Baraka did and HBO won't even show it
allow me to Ad-Lib for just a moment
"The Last Poet's must have been the last poet's"
because it's been nearly 50 years since their premier
yet the same sentiments are still continuously spoken
and as poets our English remains broken cause we only speak in pieces
write and recite bits and pieces
never peeping the entire picture we just keep spitting out pieces
now somebody please help us put this shit back together!

If seeing is believing, then show me the truth!

I want you, the listener, the observer, the reader. To take a second and open your mind, then after that open up a proverbial window, have you done so? Good! Now take everything that you believe to be true concerning the events that caused and resulted from the scripted drama of September 11th and throw that bullshit out of the window you just opened.

For you have been deceived, led to believe that a very well scripted version of
reality TV was factual, what the public got handed however dramatic were lies
and what follows might seem just a bit radical but again I must stress that you open
your mind, as I speak through the subconscious cause true indeed it all begins with a
dream
a pipe-dream, that I'll bleed black gold from the Middle East
understand that the face of the beast does not change
these are the last days and the prophesy clearly explains
that Babylon must burn in flames
so they funded the Taliban with millions in military muscle
you lay down the groundwork and then will reap the benefits
Bin Laden's already our operative, just get things into position
but the Taliban wanted a bigger percentage
(Our reaction) sand nigga please
we allowed you to breathe
now take this carpet of gold, unless you want a flying carpet of bombs dropped on
your homes, they refuse the offer
excellent, now here's our opportunity to go ahead and immediately
enact our already laid out plan, this is what needs to be understood
I think it necessary that we momentarily lurk through the 'Northwood's
let me explain, 'Project Northwood's', a very carefully pieced together blueprint
by the CIA and pentagon in 1962 to use commercial aircraft as weaponry
in which to bomb American cities, blame it on Fidel and then go get they ass
but Kennedy explicitly rejected the draft, alright cool BLAOW
blow you out of the picture with multiple sharp shooters
keep these files concealed somewhere will need them in the future
now back to the pipe dream, time to enact these schemes
before 2001 they had been getting ready for war son
load up this ammunition and target Afghanistan, Iraq and Iran
but wait, first we need a reason to strike
and the people have to believe that it's right
hmmmmm, let's take our cue from say, the 3rd Reich
propaganda comes into play, a dramatically scripted version of doomsday
Michael Moore, a he's a DJ
with vinyl made out of American soil, because he's just scratching the surface
anybody I'll tell you oils the
primary purpose
and yes the 9/11 commission is full of bullshit dead ends and contradictions
of course they knew the attacks were coming, sounds of war drumming
so they allowed it to happen, but now imagine
what if they also enacted the action?
Oh now here comes that monster creeping out of those 'Northwood's'
and he is a metaphor for war, money, destruction, death, injustice, slavery
assassination, fake emancipation
his screams are the sounds of guns busting, war drum percussion
his claws are bullets that touch the skulls of Middle Eastern children
his saliva is bombs that drop upon

innocent civilians
lasers shoot from his eyes like air crafts and crash into American buildings
with nuclear missiles attached to his shoulders
his breath blows death into the bodies of blind U.S. soldiers
and just when you thought it was over, the plot thickens
now listen, I need you to picture this deep docudrama they've written
because the version that was presented is pure fiction
the cut that got left on the pentagon editing room floor goes a little something like this
3 planes are prepared by military personnel capable of being remote controlled
1-a business jet loaded and ready to explode
2-an f-16 jet fighter and
3- a 767 painted to look like a United Airlines jet, cool the scene is set
as the four 9/11 planes featured in the official version take off the plot twist
turns while flight patterns cross as bleeps merge on radar screens and transponders are
turned off
and all three planes are instructed to
turn
off course
turn on your cell phones and send messages to your families
where under attack, but who's the enemy?
picture all four planes landing at a military base somewhere in the American mid-east
but now this is where it really gets deep
you see the 'Northwood's' demon possesses so many different complexions
however it's hard to tell his exact color due to the many possible tones of deception
but check it and peep the probable melanin method
all 3 imitation flights that crossed over and intercepted
the four official planes patterns, these represent the weaponry
first flight hits the north tower and the earth quakes
the second one hits the south tower and souls begin to shake
in the wake of an evil face the people can see fate react as buildings collapse
but wait, let's actually go back and review the facts
steel beams were supposedly melted by ignited jet fuel that had already been consumed
and fires that had previously extinguished
smoldering smoke is supposed to melt steel ridiculous
we all might as well rock *American Idiot* shirts
as more troubling questions are unearthed
how did a plane hit the south tower at an angle but melt steel beams in its interior?
why did the south tower which was hit second collapse first?
why did 90 times the stock options in the world trade get sold off so rapidly?
just days before the planes hit at amounts never before witnessed?
why did eyewitnesses escaping the madness see bombs exploding inside both towers?
only to have their testimonies appear then suddenly disappear
erased by the face of the powers that be?
why do they keep trying to hide the facts?
why did big daddy Bush have breakfast
with Bin Laden's brother on the morning of the attacks?
why did FEMA get there the night before?
and why did NORAD ignore all the signs?
or rather why were they to busy playing war games to react on time?
why were they instructed not to act?
even after it was evident that America was under attack?
Shit "why is the sky blue?
Why is water wet?
Why did Judas rat to Romans while Jesus slept?"
Babylon is burning due to extensive self-destruction
shouldn't take a rocket scientist or psychic to see exactly
who are the true culprits, this poem might as well be entitled
"Somebody Blew up America", the remix

and when the questions blend with the answers the results might make your stomach
sick
so planes crash as bombs go off inside buildings causing them to collapse
while everyone freezes to watch and it seems as if the hands of time have
stopped
a plane hits the pentagon and,
disappears
no wings, no parts, no engine, no identifiable pieces, no luggage, no corpses
but of course we're just supposed to remain in the dark and except what they tell us
with no questions asked, so when flight 93 gets shot down in Pennsylvania
eliminating living evidence to the evil plot
the general public decides to turn a blind eye and eat up the lies
with a side of freedom fries, oh it crashed in that big hole right there
even though residents of the area heard the brake in the sound barrier
from the military jets when they entered the vicinity of the airspace
BLAOW, easy, more expendable people and evidence erased
now let's analyze who exactly are the true masterminds behind the lies and
destruction they showed you 19 mysterious faces of so called Arab terrorist plastered
on your screen
leading you to believe that these are the radical fanatical Muslim fundamentalist
who committed the atrocious actions witnessed, yet get this
at least seven of them turned up still living
and four have never even been
to the United States before
and that's only from the reports that actually accidentally slipped through
Oh what a wicked plot we see has been weaved, but that ain't even the half of it
see there's much more to this mess, exactly 11 years before 9/11 on September 11 1990
Bush senior gives his
"New World Order" address
but where still not done, September 11 2002
first anniversary of the atrocity the New York City lottery
came up 911, "now how's that for a
plot twist"
big brother is watching you son and they control this shit
and at any time they are willing to send you a sign to make sure you don't forget
and that's still not it, September 11 1941
construction on the satanic pentagram known as the pentagon begun
hey yo you better listen close, they got you targeted in their scope
yea we trying to keep it alive, but there's a hit out on hope
bloody hands composed with corrupt currency stay wrapped around your throat
and to them it's just a joke
all we need is a bearded turban rocking scapegoat
and they'll believe whatever Bush-shit
we quote
even W himself said
"you can fool some of the people
all of the time, and those are the ones we want to concentrate on" end quote

so let the frames of pain, flames and burning planes
re-emerge in your brain on continuous replay
forget the lines, bars, and stanzas
this is reality laid to the page, word to
Sir Reigns
I'm spitting spoken essays, verbally mold the text until its contents visually
illustrate
they say we got an accurate identification of evils face
but wait, *D Chase* already told you that
"it doesn't take long to make a fake Bin Laden tape"
welcome to psychological warfare
the enemy is definitely an axis of evil

and its members have names like
George, Dick, Wolfowitz, Rumsfeld, Sharon, Myers, Mossad and Blair
look at the nuclear rockets' red glare, liberty bombs bursting in mid air
while mislead U.S. troops are duped into early graves
out on the front line like mind dead slaves
are you insane, Al-Qaeda ain't got shit on the CIA
not even on the same level as the Illuminati
they after small change, truck bombs and such
they ain't flying no planes, try to maintain
if Washington really wants to fight a 'war on terrorism'
all they got to do is re-aim
cock those guns and turn them towards their own brains
"so let freedom ring, with a buckshot, but not just yet
first we need to truly understand the nature of the threat"
all you need to do is review their history
principles, practices, policies and atrocious philosophies
analyzed accurately and you'll see
bloody patterns perpetrated by greedy money hungry savages
who are the most vicious consistent virus which lacks a prescription
I mean, *Mr. Mizan* already explained the aim behind the theory of
By-yo-terrorism, for it was by their terrorism
that men, women and children were labeled as less than animals and locked in chains
nearly an entire race of natives slain
and the list goes on, raping, whipping, lynching
these accounts are simply madness in motion
I'm digging deep in you'll shit, look at all the feces floating
like dead bodies in the ocean at
Pearl Harbors provoking
I found your gun mother fucker and its smoking
from multiple shots fired, at Medgar, Kennedy, Malcolm, King and so many others
now let's pack the inner city's full of
crack cocaine
and manufactured Aids, cause in order for them to remain
as those who reign, their Pyramid structure has to be sustained
the hypocrisy of democracy's deception kept intact
so they must insure that you're on the bottom floor
therefore keeping their feet on your backs
upon analyzing their history you inevitably see a common theme
terror and terrorism, executed by master terrorist
so why should we as intelligent human beings
even doubt for one minute, their abilities
to construct and perform these meticulously manufactured dramatic scenes
I mean, in currency we trust, cause when money comes into the picture
people become expendable, as *strange fruit* grows from the bloody roots of evil
they waste human lives like aqua so witness the consistent slaughter
cause obviously oil is thicker than water
its either be a prisoner or *patriot,* and I'd rather not *act*
this is real life, use fire as ink and write poetry on the stars and stripes
spewing gasoline through my windpipe, until companies are forced to drop their price
I'm asking, how many more innocent citizens and deceived U.S. military personnel
will have to be sacrificed, we've been in darkness long enough
all I'm trying to say is "let there be light"
"while black youth uses their bodies to shield bullets on blocks at night"
"Bin Laden didn't blow up the projects, it was you nigga, tell the truth nigga"
"Bush knock down the towers"
and these thoughts have opened up a
Pandora's Box
with Baraka's owl on the inside, his mind still filled with questions
but this time instead of exploding he's imploding
imploding like two towers with bombs planted on each floor

Babylon is burning I say, perfect pretext for war
just script the people a made for news movie and watch the blood pour
let the monster out of the 'Northwood's' loose
and feed him nourishment in the form of fake freedom
lies disguised as liberty and poison propaganda mislabeled as patriotism
waging an invisible 'war on terrorism' that lacks proof
sure, we think we saw
but, if seeing is believing, than show me
the truth!

The Devil's Cleansing

I do not live here
I am merely a figment of what your mind allows you to see
this is not my dimension it is only a visit
what this image exhibits only prohibits your ability to see reality
and seeing is not believing you must actually open your mind to receiving the truth
and the devil is among us

Presidents don't care about black people
even when they are black people
and it seems that my people were declassi-ficated
to the stasis of refugees when Katrina came to clean New Orleans
of its melanated population insert instant gentrification
in the form of levees braking due to explosives being ignited
at night inside the pavement
meteorologist scratching they scalps in amazement
at storm systems making sudden path changes
as a result of the eyes manipulation through weather modification
could it really be that easy?
see initially the Big Easy missed what was feared to be possibly the biggest to hit since Betsey
hurricane came and went
was near the sunshine state
yet the erased local news tapes of the broadcast that most of the gulf missed did indeed state
that in a fashion of a very irrational storm pattern practice
witness the entire system backtracking
now that's not supposed to happen
I'm talking some inorganic storm tracking magic
since when did the devil begin to specialize in unnatural disasters?
well you'd be surprised at the way Satan works inside of men's minds
engraved behind the ways of Babylon's timeline
and we are living in the last days of time
I say I say I say Ashe I say
the devil is among us

and hurricane Katrina was his version of urban cleansing
from Americas hysteria for self-inflicted Armageddon
like falling angels still clinging to heaven
intestines infected digesting Luciferian light
but then who know what the devil look like
constantly changing form directly in front of our very faces
manifesting himself in various legions of deceiving places
feeding on fear and hatred squeezed in-between his-story's erased and replaced plagiarized spaces
keeping you complacent I can't take it

the devil labeled my people refuges in New Orleans where no timely relief was sent
waiting on rooftops wading in bodies of water where bodies rot
entire communities left rent
the cost of lives lost weighed against the loss of all you own please do attempt
to maintain your souls contents
because sometimes the devil arrives in the form of your own government
no FEMA survivor retrievers or supplies sent from prayed for saints sent
and a Super Bowl won by Saints is great but still won't allow me to forget
the middle passage reenactments that resembled transatlantic slave ships
army cadets and sergeants
stacking my brothers and sisters on top of one another like
Amistad passengers
in arenas and makeshift bus stations
illustrations of what CNN and Fox News refused to broadcast on your TV stations
but what more are we to expect?
from an evil money praising nation founded by demonic masons
who slaughtered indigenous natives with smallpox laced blankets

now I bet you can't say Tuskegee Experiment 666 times fast
until it begins to resemble evangelical Christians spitting in tongues
translated into ghetto scriptures baked in crack vials and civil rights poems
loaded into a 12 years olds stolen gun
who is the great great great grandson of angels who sang freedom
while picking cotton beneath a scorching southern sun
we want our soul back

too many whip lashes splashed across our ancestors backs
to not demand truth and facts
yet it seems that our freedom songs have slowly devolved from tribal drums to "sha clack clack"
to now resembling modern day step and fetched molested over tracks
in the form of antebellum rap
sambos rocking platinum and gold in place of the shine the devil stole
we need our souls back

while the ghost of Louis Armstrong's heavenly trumpet is steady bumping
while the devil is krumping
blended with high hats and 808 percussion accompanied by hand claps
a musical production reconstructed for mass market consumption
until its function becomes disgusting
you better get your God Damn soul back

so don't ever dare refer to me like yo doesn't he rap
nigga what, this is Slangston!
spitting ancient incantations inside my cadence
while leaving ripped up pages littering stages
making the pavement beneath spiritual enslavement cave in until it cracks
my poetic mind scheme proceeds to bleed re-liquefied verses

over the surface of New Orleans' re-gentrified map
lick a shot if you want yo soul back
this was written by my ancestor's decedents while living on plantations
I was only commissioned to translate it reincarnated so I'm making contact
and this poem represents the lyrical equivalent of the Emancipation Proclamation
tattooed across Lil Wayne's back
New Orleans take your soul back

Yes I say the devil is among us
but what got forgotten is that we are God
so in remembering that the giving is why where living
you in an instant become effectively infinite at taking away all of Satan's ammunition
listen what I'm spitting isn't given as an option
one time I was in church and heard the devil next to me talking
he tried to $ell me a bible verse like it was a $lave at an auction
so I socked him in the chest
and said bitch "get yo hands out my pockets like Malcolm X"
and my soul is exploding like New Orleans levees leading to over flooding in 3rd ward projects
we saw the 3rd world right at our own door steps
and yet you telling me FEMA ain't have no more checks left
while H.A.A.R.P. instrumentation passes forth damnation on melanated populations
in the form of micro-wave gentrification
you see the word Katrina means to cleanse through the process of liquidated application
but I bet you didn't know that that the devil was in the business of baptizing inner city congregations
you see The Devil's Cleansing is what we all witnessed
but only God can purify these waters
so next time will just bring fire and may your soul be a witness
it's time for us to start getting our fucking shit back

Ashe'

Muther Fucker!

H.A.A.R.P. Strings of the God's

Heavenly sanctified hell-ified fingertips pluck upon the sacred complacent strings of the benevolent… my my such zealous incredulous of the cosmonaut zealots who construct what we deem progressive intelligence
"so all hail or get thrown towards hell"
As we collectively pale at the sounds of supreme musicianship
Behold what beautiful paintings lie in the skylines
With colors so vivid…
surely only the God's could have permitted and submitted such tinted bliss…

"Canon to the right of them
Canon to the left of them
Canon in front of them
Volley and thunder!"

yeah… whatever…

when things happen, especially atrocities of inconceivable tragedy
most people simply ask why?
Well imagine if not only did you know why?
But you also knew exactly who and how?
Brothers and sisters this is my dilemma…

In the wake of the Haiti and Chile earthquakes and the staggering amount of destruction and death
Our human nature seeks out for the creator to confess questions that rise like cancer in our chest, seeking for the answers yet few to none have come to manifest
Some would even suggest that the wrath of an almighty God has come to crush the crumbs of thee un-blessed
An all loving yet vengeful murderous God
With ways so mysterious and thy shalt not dare question this God
In reality these people know nothing of God and even less do they truly understand of thee ALL…

But now imagine if man had a plan to make himself God?
And willfully play upon the hearts of humanities sanity tragically like H.A.A.R.P. strings
of heavenly majesty holding and composing notes that orchestrate destruction so savagely
welcome to Armageddon's demented twisted biblical symphony
come and witness the scripted catastrophe
what a musical massacre of a dastardly masterpiece
as the crowd screams in demonic like agony
playing along with the doom songs of electro harmonic melody
written with fear, death, hate, greed, human need, war, plague, famine, fate, history, mystery, religion, capitalism, tyranny, all mighty democracy, mixed with hells recipes and Gods complexities as the major themes weaved into this sensationalized symphonic electronic elegized ecstasy
so you're mis-leading translations of mis-translated re-interpreted slanted ranting of re-translated apocalyptic scripture simply don't interest me
I already decoded the quotations of coded commotion once decoded by those who had coded the codes that were once eroded and exploded in the hands of those not chosen from what was written organically…

In other words believe not what you see, especially on TV…
See the H.A.A.R.P. strings of the Gods tend to bring about many things

Through the madness of electromagnetic musicality
Including hurricanes, earthquakes and tsunamis
Again I say what if man had a plan to make himself God?
Lord knows it would probably be simply written off as conspiracy

But behold this poetic documentary has a zer0.0 margin of inaccuracy
simply presenting the facts you see
for the truth cannot be edited out of view from those of us with clear 3rd ocular mobility
for they are no Gods, I see through their demonic energies
now let's review the scientific history…
in 1912 scientist Nikolai Tesla develops new complex theories in advanced radio wave frequencies and electromagnetic energy
with Tesla's technology and theories he envisioned the possibility to manipulate and control the weather's capability even claimed that eventually he'd have the ability to split the earth into 2 through the usage of high and low radio frequencies of electromagnetic technology, this later leading to a patent developed upon the foundational theories of Tesla's earlier research in 1985 by Bernard J. Eastland that would eventually transform the theories of Tesla technology into reality creating the blueprint for what is known as H.A.A.R.P. an acronym meaning High-frequency Active Aurora Research Program
a giant antenna that beams highly concentrated radio frequency energy into the upper ionosphere recreating the effects of the sun and by corresponding these frequencies with satellite signals collectively creating massive amounts of concentrated energy
the result, humankind's newest and most destructive form of weaponry
which applications include the ability to destroy incoming missiles, control and disrupt communication, weather modification as well as lift the entire ionosphere to a further location out into space to eradicate and intercept anyone's incoming position
and not that I'm trying to get too deep for some
but it seems they trying to replace the sun
or maybe their trying to replace the son
hey yo son…
again I say
what if man had a plan to make himself GOD?

"Behold the pale horse" is alive
rocking a pair of horns with fire inside his eyes
and they actually trying to rearrange the skies
radio frequencies shot into the atmosphere
in order to increase the speed of subatomic particles inside ionosphere molecules
1 billion watts of vibration-al frequencies to frequently cause the atmosphere to radiate
fire that same co density with focused electromagnetic energy into the planet and you'll manage to create arguably history's most devastating earthquake but wait…

this all probably sounds like science fiction right?
or some kind of perverted solar system mysticism
but just listen
cause see science and spiritualism are a part of the same universal coalition
for instance
the earth's atmosphere, magnetosphere and ionosphere are made up of energy
the planet energy, atoms, ions, protons, neutrons, electrons, particles, periodical elements
mineral, plant, animal life and people are energy
spirits, electricity, demonic deities, alien species, trans-dimensional technology, negative and positive thought frequencies, even the very words you recite are all energy
water, gas, electricity, micro-biology, philosophy, astrology, ecology, etymology, photography, energy
everything you both see and don't see inside the combined cipher of your daily life

are all a collective sacrifice of energy
universally condensed and expanded
all physically, mentally and spiritually situated
plus, and this is key, very capable of being manipulated
and since the energy of the people is interconnected with the energy of the planet
and both are operating on the same energy frequencies
understand this
if you can manipulate the planet
then you can just as easily manipulate the people
mind, body and soul causing various diseases, hysteria
and passivity for the purpose of population control

so yes they mos def got futuristic advanced technological weaponry
that's a definite not maybe
why you think the planet's weather patterns are constantly unnaturally so crazy
from New Orleans to the Philippians and Haiti
hey yo…
let's get a few things clear
Hurricane Katrina, the tsunami, China, Haiti, Chile and many similar sinister instances are not
merely so called natural disasters
but rather examples of electromagnetic ionospheric warfare
the same vividly colorfully consistent H.A.A.R.P. activity visually in the air
one day before the Haiti earthquake and one day before China's seismic ripper last year and the earth's-core is at warfare
due to demonically angelic hellish scientific musical compositions
composed to the pulse of your soul by secret government lab technicians
the Military Industrial dj lays the Complex track and commences to mixing
earthquakes, rain, hurricanes and aurora planes rearrange your brain into insane patterns
while masses remain mentally staggered when
H.A.A.R.P. starts to scratch on tectonic plates
with 1 billion watts of vibration-al Tesla turntablism
that turns the tables on your 3rd eye vision causing contradictions in-stereo
cause the oil they located about a year ago beneath Haiti's location
is something they not going report on your Tell-lie-vision

so forget spitting cause my convictions committed to submitting truth through the mic
cause what you have witnessed at the expense of the
Haitian nation
which just happen to be the first who achieved liberation
is another illumi-nite (knight) operation in the form of overnight gentrification
for the senseless consensus of controlling indigenous populations
while they manipulating your minds magnetite
not to mention the expensive metaphysics involved in the alchemy-tic price
in other words
another demented ritualistic sacrifice to these demonic deities in other dimensions
because Baphomet needs his nutrition, right?

and it's all energy
see everything is energy
whether viewed scientifically or spiritually it's just energy
in the form of a synergy consisting of vibration-al tendencies infinitely spinning
and the creator created the universe in accordance with the corresponding laws of rhythm
but understand that somebody keeps bumping into the fucking sound system
causing the celestial selectors record to keep skipping

Oh my God…

so again I must mention
what if man had a plan to make himself God?
and had just possibly already long since replaced
you're so called attempted contradictions that you solicit as religion
I mean how crazy would that be
but yet it seems that we have seen
Armageddon broad casted live as an episode of reality TV
As the plot proceeds to read
Like abnormal weather patterns that gather in the trees
Katrina, Haiti, The Philippians
Hurricanes, Earthquakes and Tsunamis
Extra Extra word to Tesla I bet ya they could probably split the planet like punany
just by combining the correct vibration with the resonance of the earth's pressure
and then raise the waves and increase each frequency
and you probably thinking
yo this Slangston Hughes dude and his damn poetic prophecies of doom are so far beyond me
will not really cause honestly
the chemtrails tell the tale
the matrix is real and your mind is the hell
while they blasting holes in heaven and "it ain't hard to tell"
"analyze me surprise me but can't magnetize me, scanning while they planning ways to sabotage me"
cause I can see the devil like he in 3d and the glasses came for free
but I'm not an Avatar but rather a messenger with the tri ocular ability
to separate what's fake from reality
and it feels so God to be free
cause the devil ain't got shit on me
because what you think you saw not only can I see
but metaphysically I over-stand
but I'm just saying what if man had a plan to make himself God?
Yet in actuality
In-order to find God man only needed to know himself…

Ashe'

A Poem 4 The People

They say this poetry is for the people

so lyrically I try to be the ultimate reality to their causality

verbally switching the polarity of these sesame recipes

like digesting seeds from inside weed designed by celestial means

heavenly rhyme schemes conceived from Evol alchemy

spit without needing to breathe and blow out streams of destiny

poetic pregnancy

        verbally ovulating until my conversation liquefies populations theoretically

           poems like organic telepathy

             insight a reverse verse conceptually
           instead of writing poems and verses for persons
              I write people into the poetry
            stanzas and lines upon the aging facial lines
        combine with my pages inside the sages of tangent times
                chaotic complacent minds
         incubate in think tanks and take the bait that hate provides
           metaphors medicate saliva is the serum I provide
              prescriptions from a distance
          don't catch feelings I'm next to my text just chilling
              by mic stands demanding healing
             toss thoughts watch em start flinching
       cause these darts are art "putting drug dealers out of business"

think you live catch these vibes get high niggez twitching
addicted to the diction I'm spitting
but many are missing the mission
prolific cause I see my Slanguage before I spit it

            remove your ears and place them up to the texture inside the frame
                  try to hear my pictures
              moving through traps like cerebral crack heads
             itching next to soup kitchens trying to get a scratch

my inner vision envisions an existence
where preachers and politicians
are replaced by writers painters and musicians

sure we possess our own cures living within the very curse

but won't remove sleep from eyes and awake to our own worth

                        so yea label me a speech wizard casting spit like spells
                  chanting frantic facets of pavement incantations in each verse
                              with solvents of evolved ebonics held in place
                      by panoramic views of pangaeanistic poetic placements
                                      I make it worse
as my creation shakes tectonic plates in order to reshape this very earth

Pray

I think I forgot how to pray
so I write
and this pen tells me to believe in miracles
but my words can't walk across water and neither do these worn out air forces
and if I could fly I'd probably still burn out and die because the sky's just not big enough
and most of the time I just want to shed my flesh and leave this place
and when this stage begins to resemble the same prison
as the rest of this world in which I'm leaving
where do I go to escape?
cause these pages are like enslavement disguised as liberation
and with this very art-form I have grown complacent
and somewhere between leaving her and losing her I think I lost my inspiration
"so hardcore I wrote this laying on the floor in the basement"

I mean Thelonious is nowhere to be found
Slick Vic thinks he's better than us
and Leviathan wants to kill Slangston (wait, but I'm Slangston)
in other words I have a hard time relating with myself
not to mention with others "imagine that"
internalize the shattered pieces of my complicated mind
like the unseen lines behind an abstract painting
but the sun going still rise and time still keeps us inside its containment
see I've seen this movie before
it's just the cast that keeps changing
even though the mold remains inside the same arrangement

I don't like wake up in the morning like
yea I'm going be weird and different on purpose
and ain't nobody going ever understand what I write in these verses
sometimes I kind of wish I was regular and wrote simple rhymes
that you could market on TV
but the only person who can market me is me
and even though I got 4 shadows there's only 1 me
and that's probably the reason why my money be looking so hysterical

I'm just that strange cat with the headphones and backpack
whose words be extra lyrical
but in actuality what I'm penning is truly spiritual
and sometimes when I write at night
I feel like an orphan
"this mic use to mean everything but now it seems less important"
I'm more than a poet

I'm the only person on the planet
and I think I forgot how to pray
so I write

Crack Cake

I feel like the only reason I write is for my life
and you like HipHop and clutched mics on stages at night
are my life
so because of you I need to write
writing for my life while listening to track 11
on A.T.M.'s "Writing 4 My Life"
putting pain on paper why does it feel like I can't write
in pain looking through the windows pane
crying as it pours down rain this can't be my life

you feel so good
you hurt so good
I love you
I am in love with you
In love with your smile
what I was searching for I found
with you
was a dream come true
but together we live a nightmare
but how can I be mad at you
I love you
Just want to be next to you
it hurts when you're not here
it hurts because you're right here
this is madness
like HipHop songs played on channels owned by Viacom
you make me ask what happened
how did this happen
forgive me for not knowing what wrong I've done
didn't plan on falling in love with you but now the deed is done
I need you now
just want to melt inside you
like you inside my arms the first time
me you, you me
me inside, hold me inside and freeze time
together for all time
"you make me better"
you are my never ending rhyme
A favorite poem of mine
flawed yet divine
ghetto like kool-aid with too much sugar in it
yet so so so so so so so sweet

I need you
please stop pushing me away
I fear that you love me too much
so for my love in you
you have lost all faith

I just want to see you smile again and look at me like you use to
I need you now
only happy when you're happy
I hurt when you hurt
run your hands through my hair as you sing "killing me softly"
this pain is our love
I need you now
lay with me forever
stay with me forever
I need you like good chicken and HipHop records

Pick the phone up
she won't pick the phone up
you came and gave me piece of mind
but now I just keep ripping up the pieces of my mind
why does it hurt this much to be alive
call me back like you said you would
every moment misunderstood
I wish this could be simple but this won't fit no instrumental
what are you doing to me?
why are you doing this to me?
you're killing me
hate this feeling but I'm healing quicker than Wolverine's scars when you kiss me
why did it seem better when you just missed me?
why does it feel like this?
can't hear it merits past mirage feared it I cleared it clearance parents came near it
lost in the unknown careless, fearless yet cherished I need you to hear this

baby I got your back whatever it takes
I'll rub your arms, thighs, calves, hands, feet and back whatever it takes
to make the pain go away
I need you
I believe in you
just want to hug all your pain away
I will not let you cry next to me
I'll kiss every tear away
we are mend to be God doesn't make mistakes
and baby you taste better than Crack Cake

baby maybe I just can't love you the right way
I wish I could write all the pain of your life away
God please give me the strength to take all the pain away
take every scar every bruise every ache
every scream every care every tear every rape
and if nobody else cares baby I do
you smell like possibilities
I feel my future inside you

look at me
you are so beautiful
please talk to me
we need to communicate
why are you doing this to me?
I love you

God why does it hurt so much
I need you
It feels so good but hurts so much
It hurts so good to love you this much
I pray for your touch
the opposite of lust
the pain of your love
this love is like pain
it hurts so much to love you this much

not to be continued...

Mind Wine

Imagine if you could walk on the sun
well for 7 days I did
probably got too close too quick
but I wouldn't trade the experience regardless
of how intense the rays get cause you be that shit
that good shit

forget being cautious I'm tossing that to the wind
and they say mixing love with friendship is dangerous
but right now my middle name is fuck that shit

and though it may sound like it
it's really not that deep
cause we simply connect like
like rhyme to beat or grind to street
no like the lines in this piece
couldn't find the right words
so instead I tried to write
these words and speak
translations through Slangston's pen

but you mean so much more than just poetry to me
and really I just want to give you reason to smile again at 6am
so taken in by the way she seems to descend and glide through rooms

sweeter than the sweetest taboo
consistent and addictive cause even "crack cake" ain't got nothing on you

your smile makes me want to freestyle myself into a coma
just so I could dream about you

composing vibrant colors with a designers touch
sunshine combined with rain you got me inspired now
cause shorty always holds me down
like good memories when the days get rough
enough
there is no equal
the perfect mixture of ghetto and griot
walking with balance in her credo
B-girl to the neo with more vision than coleco
and it's so cool how you think
all the corny shit I say
is so sweet
but peep

the only reason you probably ever saw light in me
was most likely due to the reflection of you

so when I'm near you it naturally brings out the best in me

yea I walked on the sun
but fail short of its shine
was too busy thinking with my head instead of my head
and went blind
so on that note I got to quote Aquil Mizan
"my bad, I apologize"
cause like that song by the Jackson 5
"I want you back" and that's a fact

I now see beyond the pussy between your thighs
would rather liquefy your aquarianinity mentally
specifically described
as you conversing and converting my calligraphy into cursive
her cerebral cervix reworking my universes purpose
through true verses
sick enough to stop time

want to feed you food for thought while we sip on Mind Wine
from now on into our next lifetime

and around then is when I felt myself falling
falling in love with you
but I don't have any wings

and the ground that most men walk on
isn't grounded enough to break my fall
so I just hold on to the hope that an Angel
will come catch me

Deferred Dreams (Soliloquy of a Quiet Nightmare)

"What happens to a dream deferred" or even worse a quiet nightmare disturbed.

Awoken from within itself, silence broken spoken like a gunshot quoted through the mouth of a sniper's barrel in Memphis.
You see the dream was murdered on a balcony in 1968 and it's my consensus that ya'll niggez is still sleep, content in your own slumber.
I Wonder what Martin would say today if he was still breathing to bamboozled spooks money scheming and slaves masquerading as Gangsters American dreaming trigger squeezing wit they eyes wide shut.
As the screaming silence of Kings so called followers ripple with deafening echoes through time at frequencies much louder than the actual outspoken words of his enemies could ever even touch. WAKE UP!
We just a bunch of niggez dreaming, WAKE UP!

Cause ya'll niggez is niggez, no not niggez but I mean niggez.
Living with your third eye on dim, making Martins sacrifice look worthless due to your action-less actions packing gats moving crack and routinely reenacting Wyllie Lynch.
Ya'll I smell the stench of niggez
quite sleeping nightmare breeding self-inflicted wound bleeding niggez.
Yo fuck your insecurities I'm exercising the authority to expose you to yourself nigga.
Cause this is much bigger than your bars about cars and bitches
or even your corner office, white wife, upper class riches and house with picket fences.
And like an injection from a weapon that's lethal through lack of unity niggez rape their own people and devourer whole communities then actually have the audacity to start bitching, like yo son, "stop snitching."
That's why the retention of our conscious conviction has been relentlessly rocked
While the majority of so called black leaders just be sleepers who do nothing but talk
And if King was to come back right now he'd probably say fuck ya'll niggez
And bounce to Canada like in that episode of The Boondocks
While America and the media tries to minimize the man and the vision
to the size of a box, oh he had a dream and then he got shot
but don't look so shocked
because when dreams become deferred they often turn into nightmares
and King's Dream has long since festered and exploded into a living life-mare
WAKE UP!

And the saga of lies and deception that I was sent to unravel plays like a modern Hollywood spy flick edition insisting that America begins to finally look at their own reflection, while they continue to present reality TV in the form of a history lesson.

Chapter One: A small time thief and x army cadet with a bad shot named James Earl Ray gets a rifle from a mysterious man known only as "Raul"
Chapter Two: Around 6pm April 4th 1968 Ray located in a bath house across from Kings Motel room miraculously manages to balance himself on the seal of a bathtub, aim one perfect shot with sniper perfection out of a window through a foliage filled tree and directly into Kings head.
Now turn the page as oh so conveniently Ray decides to leave a bag of his belongings along with the murder weapon, littered with his fingerprints, in front of a store right near the crime scene.

Next Chapter: The only positive Id of Ray at the scene came from a man so wasted the cab driver wouldn't even pick him up, and then he later rein-canted the statement. Now check down to the next passage for even more move faking.
James Earl Ray's confession in which he subsequently withdrew almost instantly was forced out of him by his very own attorney when Percy threatened him with the death penalty.

Hey yo they must think we either stupid or half crazy
These fraudulent chapters do not present History
But rather His-Story
In the form of deception lies and lunacy
So you're halfhearted apologies for Jim Crow and slavery
Ain't even got the slightest opportunity of even remotely moving me
In other words, get the fuck out my face with that bullshit
Cause the evidence, or lack thereof that you present
Reads like the poorly written script of some wack ass movie
This is no longer poetry but rather spoken realism spitten with intensity
Visually producing like I chewed up the Willie Lynch papers and the United States Constitution and vocally starting shooting a documentary.
So listen to these words I speak as truth shall leak
Through mental cracks wire taps and hate speech
It gets deep like the remains of Babylonian streets
Dug from beneath
but you already know the nature of the beast
so peep…

COINTELPRO Or rather the counter intelligence program
was created and initiated by the SOG Seat Of Government
aka J Edgar Hoover and the FBI
in order to target and discredit black leaders amongst their
own kind
through the dissemination of incriminating misinformation and lies
specifically targeted at the time, were any potential black Messiah's
with the power to move minds provoking black people to unify
and electrify the militant Black Nationalist movement
so four particular individuals were identified
Malcolm, Elijah, Stokely and King

However King was the most difficult to deal with due to his tactics
and unwavering stance of non-violence
but what really did it, is that King started challenging the structure
of imperialisms pyramid
and when you do that you in an instant become a liability they can't risk
don't believe me, see Robert and John F. Kennedy for more on that shit
I mean just imagine this, President Robert Kennedy and Vice President
Martin L. King
Yes, believe me, it was poised to happen
in the words of William F. Pepper

"For one bright moment back there in the late 1960s we actually believed that we could change our country. We had identified the enemy. We saw it up close and we had its measure -- and we were very hopeful that we would prevail .. Then suddenly, All our dreams were instantly gone, destroyed by an assassin's bullet."
so sure they can have their little civil rights
appease them with pretend integration a voting card and the mirage of a choice
between evil and evil, cause as long as you control the distribution of wealth
the people on the bottom shelf remain fucked
but don't give them any knowledge or nutrients
like land or investments, just supply them with a ballot and some entertainment
in the form of a pacifier to suck
But you see Martin understood this and initiated an initiative
to organize the masses piece by piece through peace
in demanding the immediate redistribution of capitol and cash flow
in-order to alleviate

enslavement and poverty across the globe and in doing so
through the scope of the enemy eventually became intolerable
so they devised and applied pressure from all sides
and the instructions handed down were simply
"that nigger isn't to leave Memphis alive"
so the coalition was given "Orders to Kill" by the shadow government
in which to bring about "A Murder in Memphis"
take out the one "Code Named Zorro"
and just in case put in place about "Three Assassins" to handle it
contracted mafia mercenaries in the bushes along with Memphis police in position

"quite early the next morning around 8 or 9 o'clock, all of the bushes and brush on the hill were cut down and cleaned up. It was as though the entire area of the bushes from behind the rooming house had been cleared . . ."

plus trained US Militia forces perched
like birds of death on top of the pent house across from it
with James Earl Ray as the unknowing patsy undisclosed in a separate location
set up perfectly to take the wrap for the shit
then feed the media a story that's somewhat miraculous

"James Earl Ray had fired the shot from the bathroom on that second floor, come down that hallway into his room and carefully packed that box, tied it up, then had proceeded across the walkway the length of the building to the back where that stair from that door came up, had come down the stairs out the door, placed the Browning box containing the rifle and the radio there in the Canipe entryway." Then Ray presumably got in his car seconds before the police's arrival, driving from downtown Memphis to Atlanta unchallenged in his white Mustang."

rushed from the bathhouse to the escape car
more than a block away in only two minutes
and somehow left behind a nice neatly packaged bag
filled with all the evidence

"However Hanes testified that in the summer of 1968 he interviewed Guy Canipe, owner of the Canipe Amusement Company. Canipe was a witness to a Memphis Police Officer dropping in his doorway the bundle that held a trove of James Earl Ray memorabilia, including the rifle, unfired bullets, and a radio with Ray's prison identification number on it."

plus I find it strange how when King was transferred to the
Lorraine Motel
he was unknowingly moved from the first to the second floor
near the balcony at the last minute.
not to mention all of his police protection was suspiciously removed
on the very day of the incident.
so now view the facts for yourself
because it's high time that we awake honestly
and when the shot rang out and fingers pointed
the direction was more like misdirection
please don't believe the hype

"There were two photographers on the roof of the Fire Station and they filmed everything. They were still cameramen and they filmed the balcony, the shot hitting King, the parking lot, up into the bushes and they got the sniper just lowering his rifle."

just peep each photo and analyze their geometry
the trajectories misleading believe me
cause clues to the truth lies or rather the true lies lies

right in-front of your eyes inside the picture
were you'll witness a foul most flagrant
the man kneeling beside King seconds after the shot
is named Merrell McCullough
a police informant slash undercover CIA agent
right there on the scene of the crime, amazing
but peep this, when one Ms. Grace Stephens
told Authorities that James Earl Ray
was without a doubt not the man she witnessed
they locked her up inside a mental institution in nearly an instant
doesn't surprise me, because in Amerikkka you either end up dead
or labeled crazy for speaking the truth
However I speak it with force and refuse to retort my recital
and the sickest consensus against the official evidence
all ballistics taken from Ray's rifle
have yet to ever match the bullet taken from King

"the actual murder weapon has been lying "at the bottom of the Mississippi River for over thirty-one years."

and yet whole when removed somehow now exits
inside fake pics where it sits in pieces
broken like the crack that has forever sat within Amerikkkas
murderous mirage of so called liberty
one nation under imperialism literally
from a fascist state of united snakes
this is not a debate the matrix has been erased
to recreate your fake history.
So who actually deserves the responsibility?
Who deserves the blame for the shot and the aim?
Who stood to gain, well fuck the assumptions
and that bullshit rhetoric you keep bumping
how about I just go ahead and name names.

Earl Clark, Merrell McCullough, Percy Forman, David Garrow, Ramsey Clark, George McMillan, Jeremiah O' Leary, Richard Billings, Priscilla Johnson McMillan, Gerald Posner, G. Robert Blakey, Clyde Tolson, Carthy Deloach, Gerald Frank, Bill Edison, Lloyd Jowers, David Burnham, James McCloud, George Landner, Claw Shaw, Frank Liberto, Carlos Marcello, William Schaap, J.D. Hill, The Phoenix Operation, Special Forces Alpha 184, the 111th and 902nd military intelligence groups, The Invaders, James McCraw, John Campbell, Dick Billings, C.D. Jackson, Donald Jameson, Donald Wilson, Evan Thomas, William Manchester, The Warren Commission, the HSCA, Jesse Jackson, Steve Tompkins, Bob Woodward, Richard Helms, Sen. Robert Byrd, Sen. James O. Eastland, Richardson Preyer, E. Howard Hunt, William Bradford Huie, Arthur Hanes, "Raul", the FBI, the CIA, contracted mafia hit-men, the Memphis Tennessee Police Dept., COINTELPRO,
J. Edgar Hoover, President Lyndon B. Johnson, and a voluntarily blinded United States Government. Need I go on, I spit the Slanguage Arts so you can do the math on your own.

While the mass media monster manages to manipulate minds at a miraculous rate
We as the human race continue to sleep late, DREAMING
content to exist inside a quite nightmare of complacency and compromise
open your eyes, open your mind
and you just might find something bigger than yourself
that's what King realized and visualized a Nobel Prize much greater than wealth
beyond material but materialized through giving of self
but we can't see that vision because our eyes are shut
while minds remain stuck in a state of unconsciousness
including confusion through unprogressive circular movements inside DREAMS
and to me that's as useless and stupid as Hillary Clinton daring to quote King

well as for myself, I refuse to DREAM
that's write, I will not DREAM

cause my eyes are open and my mind is awake
spitting truth like *Thunder* from my *Mouth*
provoking earth quakes, for heaven's sake
cause each verse I create is meant to make pens penetrate
and demonstrate ways to innovate as thoughts collaborate
even if I have to lyrically shake people awake
cause this is beyond four words and a holiday to commemorate
a DREAM that has deferred far past its expiration date WAKE UP!
we have nothing to celebrate
"It's like we live in the United States of Amnesia"
moving with murdered memories sleeping through life
and somewhere along the way forgot about those who sacrificed
hypnotized by spinning rims and blinded with excessive amounts of ice
STOP DREAMING…

I mean King must have been trapped in a DREAM in order to believe
that true **change** was something we could actually achieve
or maybe he was so far ahead of his time, that even now
we remain blind to the content of what his vision truly means
much deeper than race, the roots of these United States
are drenched in blood death and greed, fueled by seeds of hate
but as long as you remain asleep they will allow you to DREAM

BET a DREAM, MTV a DREAM, CNN, NBC and FOX News all silently asleep
NAACP you're DREAMING
Al Sharpton, Jesse Jackson, Colin Powell, Condoleezza your DREAMING
Barak Obama, whatever nigga, your DREAMING

Like the vivid day-mares of a stillborn fetus trapped inside the womb of life
whose mouth will never breathe the breath of reality
we walk silently
awake while DREAMING

On April 4th 1968 at 6:01pm on a motel balcony in
Memphis Tennessee
Dr. Martin Luther King Jr. was murdered, assassinated
by the same government
that now commemorates him with a holiday
dying along with him, his DREAM
yet no one woke up, no one pick the torch up
like we all just closed our eyes and laid back
in deep slumber DREAMING
waiting for Martin Luther King to come back
while almost every Boulevard that bares his name
is nearly as violent as Iraq
and over 40 years after his death we remain Deferred by a dead DREAM
that silently sleeps inside the comfortable confines of a Quite Nightmare

Now who's brave enough to WAKE UP?

A Dude Playing A Dude Pretending To Be Another Dude
a.k.a.Obama-Nation(Part 1, The Post Modern Coup)

So, this is what we been waiting for and this is what so many risked their lives and died for, a face-lift/ an imperialist facelift, this is it
Some kind of Masonic messiah makeshift reading from Brzezinski's transcript really, this is it, are you serious, I cannot actually be hearing this
But some of ya'll, well most of ya'll, aight lets just be honest most likely all of yall, then fallen/ like Icarus drifting over the skyline at noontime hung over on his own perverted tonic diverted from the minds un-sober promise, both "right" and "left" wing burning in flames just the same from getting to close to the sun yet still we decide to ride one
Burning like dry papyrus in the fire of a liars lesser evil, as if one actually existed
And if it was lesser, that wouldn't mean that the devil hadn't invested in it either
Satan's left jab ain't no weaker than his right, ya'll need to seek the light
Words spoken as hopeless and anti-potent as castrated husbands making attempts at fucking they wife, but simply are not aiding in the production of life
But see preacher's politicians and poets keep hugging the mic and blogging at night
Go back to the drawing board and reverse let's say a smorgasbord of the nonsense that you write, slaves rocking heavy chains talking about freedom when they recite
Some of the most conscious talking activist and artist they have all fallen, willingly like bungee jumpers and spring pollen awake with eyes closed walking into wide open coffins
While Sam Cooke is in his grave tossing and throwing tantrums, screaming this can't be the CHANGE coming that I had imagined
See they then stole the 40 acres and put the mule inside the master's mansion, madness!
Some demo-republacratic erratic fanatic post traumatic slave rations, passed off as new millennium magic, the title of Marvin's most celebrated classic needs to be renamed from "what's going on" to "people what the flying fuck is happening"
While bamboozled crowds keep clapping at the same speech every day of the week
But then again what I'm I saying, most of ya'll thought that Bill " Rocke-criminal-feller " Clinton was the man, so who the hell I'm I asking
Hocus pocus ya'll don't know this or seem to notice
But centuries of hypocrisy cannot be instantly erased as easily and simply as he got melanin, so now we win, so now we win, so now we win
To quote Chuck D, "this ain't the Super Bowl"
Plus quarterbacks don't own the team my friend
But some of ya'll actually believe that things can CHANGE overnight from the 4th to the 5th just because somebody with black skin
got in
Pretend politriks got the masses duped by the Post Modern Coup
In this blood filled melting pot they trying to pass off as
American Soup
But something fucking smells in the kitchen
Listen they been cooking up these same deranged recipes from the beginning, Imperialism and Capitalism with the perfect perverted mix of Satanism and Masonic symbolism/but the kool-aid they presenting is so damn delicious "oh yea" so we just keep sipping/ "yes we can" now throw in some **skulls** and **bones** with sheepeople on the frontline like mindless drones/ For ages you got the same bloodlines with their behinds well shown to the throne/ It shouldn't even be a surprise, the genealogy they don't even try to hide it's easy/ just analyze the family tree and its venomous vines Bush, Cheney, Clinton, Hillary, Kerry, Obama, Palin, Lincoln, Queen Elizabeth, Prince Charles, Princess Dia, they are all related DNA integrated
"I'd like to know what info those who voted researched and investigated
Independently of mainstream media's spoon fed doses of lies and spin

It's sad and amazing that the most skeptic of the population
Those of us who should be the most vigilant in our politics
Have been the most easily led to the slaughter
And that is not divisive, that is the truth"
and I will "continue to tell the truth even at the risk of
being verbally lynched by those who want me to share in a delusion
if you think that Barack is going to reverse what W.
did you are kidding
no phony drug war, spy satellites
warrant-less wiretaps, the Patriot Act
none of it will be reversed with this corporate stunt
Hoax of an election, fact
His foreign advisor created Al Qaeda, the muhajadeen
Did anyone who voted research that?
Did anyone research his VP
Biden meeting with the ISIS chief
Or ordered the $100,000 wired to Mohammed Atta?"
Two sides of the same whole, at odds on how to keep control of the human crop
I ask you, where does the hypocrisy stop, answer, it doesn't
Why would it, when it works so well
I mean people are happy right, people are content in their slavery
I mean we complain like all hell about how awful shit smells
But nobody wants to actually get their hands dirty cleaning the toilet
So they keep you nice and occupied with the crumbs
And why would I even be surprised, shit fam I'm a slave like you
Need good health care and a place to lay my head just like you
Just keep the masses detracted through the madness that these governing men continue to create, and when they at their lowest point manufacture them a hero with a familiar looking face, a giant O on his chest and a synthetic rhetoric laced cape
But make no mistake, I over-stand the plight of your blind sight
Cause how we going be concerned with freedom when we concerned with eating
Food prices is high as shit, gas expensive then a bitch
Fuck freedom we need life insurance, fuck freedom we need doe to pay off car notes
Mortgage is a muther fucker plus Wall Street got peeps losing they homes
Freedom ain't free people
Whole economy fucked like a 10 dollar ho so yea I know
Cause living free ain't that simple
"see what I see and see that freedom ain't free"
Fuck freedom niggez need roofs over heads, clothes to wear and mandated health care
So it seems freedom ain't essential if survival is a must, plus you know what
We ain't really concerned with nobody but us, but hold up
How many of us are actually informed about the facts, or did you cast a ballot simply off the fact that he's black, now let's examine that
Ancestors bleed and died for this so called right, so to cast a vote, without knowing
Why, who or what the fuck you're voting for is thee equivalent
Of spitting in the face of their plight, it is not right, no fuck that
"It ain't right"/ you might as well take a shit on the graves of hung slaves
Nigga you best keep a close watch, it's like somebody got you for your watch
Cause niggez don't know what time it is!
But oh wait, he's the one, so since he gets in we all won, because he won
cause he's the one
And this is what we all been waiting for and he won
The one, our son, a black skinned man has run and he won cause he's the one
And since he wins we all won, Hosanna Obama my grandmamma thought she'd never live to see the coming of the one, but behold there he stands
At the podium of this great land with hope in his hand
Don't ya'll understand this man has the plan
To unite black, brown, yellow and white in the fight to save all mankind
Don't you understand, it's like, he's got the whole wide world in his hand
Obama is the man, shame on you if you don't understand

And you must be hating, you got to be hating, if you can't get with the plan
Cause he's a Blackman, you know what I'm saying
You know how long we been waiting for this, come on black people stop playing and vote for the man, and then we'll just HOPE that he's the one
The one, like we been saying, Hosanna Obama
The son of a Caucasian American and African, so that makes him an African American
And he's a black man, so come on black people, get with the program
He's here to save and CHANGE this wretched land, so we could all be Americans
"A better tomorrow is at hand"
And ya'll actually believed that shit, Barack Obama ain't fucking Jesus bitch
Oh but he's the one, oh but he's the one, the one, we been waiting so long for just that one/ Who could actually get it done, yo let me tell you something about the so called one
Recruited by Zbigniew Brzezinski in 1981 at Columbia University
Because of his intelligent charismatic ability, racial versatility and most importantly
His elite Draconian pedigree, but I'm a try not to go too deep
Let's stick to the basics why don't we
you may be asking who the hell is Zbigniew Brzezinski / a powerful muther fucker that's co-founder of the Triladal Commission along with David Rockefeller, no not Jay-z muther fuckers the real Rockefeller
ZB who he be, big banker plus global gangster one of the top political pranksters
Master mind weaving deceitful designs worldwide Illuminized global genocide a million times multiplied version of John Gotti responsible for nearly a billion bodies one of the elite financial commanding chiefs in the illuminati, agent of CHANGE here to save hardly, simply more of the same? Most logically
10 times worse than bumbling Bush lead neo-cons who bomb little countries that can't respond properly, probably, now obviously something just doesn't add up
You see Brzezinski is the head foreign policy adviser to Barack
But this shouldn't be no shock, for starters this is the same cat who recruited and backed Jimmy Carter, cause when it comes to politics this is what you got
To parts of the same whole, democrat republican, the only real debate is over how to keep control, of you, the sheeple, there are no lesser degrees of evil
You see the people behind Barack like Brzezinski and the CFR are nothing more than Illuminati pawns, no different from the neo-cons, all tools for oppressions right arm
Hillary, McCain, Palin, Biden, Obama all members of the same squad
So how can I respond to more rhetoric, politriks and utter nonsense
Making your ballot a disguise for more bondage, with ourselves we need to be honest
I mean the shit is fucking up noxious, Obama can't nor does he want to CHANGE the system responsible for his political production, you're bugging
Unable to see the true lies that lie in plain sight, its nothing
Dude ain't even effectively bluffing, but we don't even listen or engage in the research
Just take the bait of the keywords, in debates where candidates only conversate about so called policies but never discuss what sits beneath the surface
The media is worthless, keeping you off point on purpose is they purpose
And I'm sick of the bullshit they keep blurting out they mouths, are you serious
Neither of these candidates give a shit, nor are they supposed to, that's not what they're here for/ they're here for more oppression imperialism and war
Sure, with Barack in office we won't be fighting in Iraq and Iran no more
But instead we going keep bombing Pakistan, put more troops in Afghanistan and most likely invade Sudan, not because of humanity but tragically to cut off China's oil supply
Causing them to clash with the Soviets in an attempt to make the United Snakes the only remaining superpower on the map, Imperialisms new agenda backed by war
And more death, more troops with their lives left wasted like leaders of spilled water in Middle Eastern deserts, while the elite feast off of our suffering
And continue to profit from the pain of the poor, and that's something I can't ignore
Look at how much blood has already been poured, they get rich off wars
So how the fuck can you be so sure, that Obama represents CHANGE, its bullshit

He's more of the same, different face same imperialist agenda, just a different plot, with the same goal, with a colored face, under a different name
But we are just slaves, and he is not CHANGE
No I'm not hating, I'm truth displaying and soothsaying
Potent political poetry smothering pages until the ink clots
Of course McCain equals more of the same
but what proof has been displayed that would make you think that Obama does not
you don't know that nigga, don't know shit about him
except for the limited view that the media permits viewable through your tell-lie-vision
telling lies to your vision, making third eyes all but non-existent
think about how crazy that is, casting a vote for someone you truly know absolutely nothing about/ that is fucking scary/ and you don't know this dude
allow me to allude, to Robert Downey Jr's character it Tropical Thunder
cause this dude, is a dude playing a dude pretending to be another dude, he ain't the one
he's the one, a fucking mulatto puppet for the Trilateral Commission, CFR, The Bilderbergs, Zbigniew Brzezinski, George Soros and all them other clicks of imperialist and real American Terrorist criminal capitalist dudes, so what the fuck makes you think that dude gives a fuck about you, dude is here cause of them, not you, but everybody seems to be fooled
by the oh so eloquent speech of the puppet on the tube, and they got they eyes glued, it's an illusion my dude, of the dude playing a dude pretending to be another dude
an illuminist under the illusionist solution of a Democrat fronting as an honest politician
as if such a thing actually existed, inside a 2 party system, you got to be kidding
do not underestimate the vicious intentions of these United Snakes, cause like Da La the stakes are too high, to be misconstrued
but we all fall for the damm okie doke of these bullshit political feuds
we eat the filthy crumbs that have fallen from the table while they consume all the real food/ so desperate in our desperation that we have been blinded by false HOPE
fallen under the yoke confused, so fuck it, he black and talk good
and says everything that I'm conditioned to think I want to hear
so cool, let's all fall into the trap that has been construed
and go vote for the dude playing a dude pretending to be another dude
put into power by the real powerful dudes
crazy how we throw all of our everything behind some candidate and I don't care what candidate it is either, it makes no sense, are you retarded, you don't know this nigga
yet some of our most promising supposedly conscious artist and activist have fallen for The Coup, continually duped into carrying out the will of the elite
thinking something's going CHANGE because somebody of a different race takes the seat, it is evident that we have been oppressed into a deep sleep
and it is fucking disgusting, I mean thee audacity, thee audacity
cats rocking iced out Obama t-shirts with fucking buttons attached
have no idea who's pulling the strings at his back, thee audacity
you have no idea the horror we facing, yet niggez been changing the names on they fucking myspace's and sending out numerous e-mails and text messages/you actually got niggez fasting and producing elaborate power point presentations with people in pictures flashing the illuminati singles with they hands/ right in front of our faces in plain sight, yet we are still to blind to see let alone over-stand/ Hosanna Obama, but if only they knew what was really upon us/ try to imagine the audacity of these secret people in power
got us eating out they fucking hands like birds, it's absurd
the audacity, they then reduced humanity to sheeple
the audacity, of us to think that something would actually CHANGE
fucking insanity, so obviously these got to be the last days
and the prophesy clearly explains, that as a people we are on the wrong page

worse than slaves, we have become in caged victims inside a system that carries out
the mission of complacent bondage, using our own fears, faith, dreams, greed, pleads
and needs on us, by giving us a front in the form of what we think we want
one of our own dudes, who's really a dude playing a dude pretending to be another
dude
how easily we have been fooled, the audacity, the fucking audacity of these cats
actually
claiming that MLK's Dream has come true, you are confused
the fucking audacity, listen to me, people please do not!!!
irrationally compare fucking Barack Obama to Martin Luther King or Malcolm X
the fucking audacity of this dude, who's really a dude
playing a dude pretending to be another dude, they fronting
cause dude is the fucking oppressors most beautifully painted puppet
the most brilliant and potentially most destructive puppet
that imperialism has ever constructed
genius, absolute genius, and it worked, better than they ever could have HOPED or
imagined, political football ya'll
play action, fake the run to Hillary Clinton
pump fake to McCain, then deep pass down the middle to Barack Obama
and we ain't have no fucking free safety in the game
instead he got replaced with HOPE, so fuck a defense
cause all we got left to defend is an impotent vote
but there is a clear difference between being an optimist and being ignorant
but unfortunately optimism and ignorance often coexist
"and condemnation without investigation is the height of ignorance"
"while dissent is the highest form of Patriotism"
and imperialism has been given a face lift
imperialism now has a black face, imperialism in black face imperialism is in black
face
the audacity, cosmetic political surgery, people there is no lesser evil
"we are the change we've been waiting for"
yes there are lots of good people still in this world
but in terms of the people who control it, there are none
so what makes you think that he would be the only one
the one, this dude playing a dude pretending to be another dude
an illuminist puppet playing the role of positive progressive politician pretending
to be a different kind of democrat, how is it that we fail for that
easy, it's nothing to it, just give the same hypocrisy from the last 20 centuries a
new look, the audacity, cosmetic political slavery, I mean surgery, well actually its
all the same you see, methodically let us make a **Manchurian Candidate**
and it has worked to a beautiful perfection, what an immaculate eloquent speaking
weapon/and the result will be a world tragedy the likes that we have never seen to
this day/evoking a price on human life that merely CHANGE cannot pay
and unfounded HOPE will not match it
because imperialism has successfully been given a facelift
just more politricks, continuing to perpetuate the agenda of these domestic American
Terrorist/funded by big banking illuminist, yea, basically they fooled you bitch
because imperialism has been given a
nice neat facelift, and I would rather have my fucking hands chopped off with a God
Damn hatchet then cast a ballot in support of that shit
so in closing just let me say this
fuck Washington, Adams and fuck Jefferson, plus Madison, Monroe and the other Adams,
fuck Jackson, Van Buren, Harrison, Tyler, Polk, Taylor, Fillmore, Pierce and
Buchanan, Fuck Lincoln, Johnson, Grant, Hayes, Garfield, Arthur, Harrison, Cleveland
and McKinley
fuck Roosevelt, Taft, Wilson, Harding and Coolidge, fuck Hoover, Fuck Franklin
Roosevelt, fuck Truman, fuck Eisenhower, fuck Kennedy, Johnson and Nixon, Ford,
Carter and Reagan, fuck Bush, fuck Clinton, fuck Bush again and Fuck Obama
now I audaciously HOPE, that you exercised your right to vote on that historic
Tuesday

let us pray, let us pray, that even through Satan's most evil intentions, the most high's mission is only strengthened, Ashe!

Italic= words of Ashante Ashante

Obama-Nation Part 2 (Imperialism's True Face Revealed)

My president is black, my vision is too
he got melanin and so do me and you
so that must mean that the sky's no longer blue
racism is dead super Negro to the rescue

so just who exactly is the mulatto messiah?
poker faced stoker of the financial fires
the truth 2 the liars
the way and the light with the might
the 666 viro chip to the Vatican empire
Hmmmmmm...

OBAMA
or at least that's what the brothers was shouting in the streets on the eve of inauguration
on the that day labeled as being so historical
as if it was prophesied from the skies by an oracle
all hail to the free world's newest CEO
the plantation spoke folk is a house Negro
the ghost of a ghost who was supposedly a spook who they sat by they own door
while we was patiently waiting and anticipating liberating changes
the true owners and holders of the Amero Euro stock that we'll never own
was busy rearranging the globe
while mentally strengthening slavery's ubiquitous strong hold

you see Americas not a nation but rather a corporation
and every single president is seen as simply a temporary CEO
and in the gods of money hungry lust and iniquitous capitalist illuminist
skulls and death surrounded by bones is what they trust
by any means needed to keep you feeding from the bottom of the totem pole
Presidents aren't elected but rather preselected
therefore a ballot and a vote is like a body with no soul
Dead!
and democracy died a long time ago
and it's definitely no different in the case of Mr. Soetoro
oh wait, what is that ya'll call him B.H.O.
Barack Hussein Obama
actually born Barry Soetoro
as written on his actual birth certificate printed in Kenya

now please do proceed to keep your minds open
see you don't need to be a citizen to be a president when you're chosen
but chosen by who?
is the question
you see the same 13 families control the globe
manipulate the souls and harbor all the gold
and if you retrace the bloodlines all roads still lead to Rome
a New World Order build on the foundation of melanated peoples slaughter all across the globe
so how do you now maintain that control

easy
galvanize them by supplying them with one of their own
because what we're dealing with are the descendants of the exact same imperialistic delegates
who initiated the institution of slavery upon the mother continent
and brought our ancestors here in slave ships
and ain't nothing new under the sun
cause they daughters and they sons are on the same shit
only difference is your brain stays locked in the chains while you've become numb to the whip
but niggez don't know shit
niggez don't know shit

yo we running out of time it's not out of spite that I write this
I'm typing to enlighten but my people are too content
with table scraps and swine in the form of health care plans
and stimulus packages to open they mind blind to the politricks
and that shit ain't even the tip of the ice burgs drip
but if I really gave you the truth it would probably cause your dome to split
so just stop reading this, please stop reading this
go back to bumping your Gucci disk
or watching Beyonce and Gaga strip
as oppose to being concerned with what's going on in places like the Gaza Strip
one of the saddest days of my life
was watching my people forget why they fight
shedding tears on election night
behaving adjacent to the containment of their enslavement
completely oblivious content with a slice of a pie baked in shit
so basically Harriet Tubman should of just slit her wrist
cause Nat Turner wasn't fighting for this
Fredrick Douglass wasn't writing for this
Marcus Garvey wasn't sparking our collective consciousness for the result to be this

And now it seems that the euphoria of the his-toric inauguration has dissipated
didn't take long for hope and change to get evaporated and re-precipitated
as the same old lack of action and participation in mapping out our own destinations
while the World Bank was jack faking and orchestrating an instigated
financial apocalypse for the ages

now here's where the road splits
there's a reason why nobodies retrieving any of the documents
let's retrace what's been erased its common place once you investigate
because spooks aren't meant to exist… oh shit
so who or what are we dealing with?

drifting through the messes of recession and financial Armageddon it's nonsense if you guessing
that economics has anything to do with a President
when it's the World Bank, Federal Reserve and Jesuits
who set the financial precedent for dead presidents
and if the CEO walks out of line in an attempt to step to this
they'll end up just like Lincoln and Kennedy did
as DEAD Presidents

the government doesn't control shit
they just manage it, word to Kris
Presidents are merely the equivalent of a manager at Mickey D's
please do believe the truth, while they can reimburse or disperse financial stimuli

in exchange for cold fries
they cannot supply anything new on the menu nor do they want to
besides they'd only get fired or rather fired upon if they tried to

but here's what they will do
implode the dollar price over a course of 5 years
then buy up all the top shares
followed by distribution of cross market movement
while the top banking executives purposely ignore all the warnings
and speculative red flags engaging in bloody money hungry
back handed finances
pretending in front of the mass public that the collapses we're caused by merely ignorance
when in reality it had nothing to do with inflated mortgages
but rather the excessive collected market derivatives
another orchestrated implosion of a senseless slave minded barter system
to manipulate the sheeple into a state of helplessness and oppression
exact same tactic enacted in the great depression
and all they needed to deceive us was the perfect puppet I mean spokesmen
for big banking invested investments in the form of a President
to accurately keep the masses distracted from the actual deception but check it
the real question is exactly who or what is truly behind it all

you see it doesn't really matter
because desiring the truth and actually being able to handle it
are two completely different matters
your minds not ready, your imagination can't effectively gather the right matter
your thoughts I'll probably splatter up against the walls of your mental and metaphysical
trance dimensional tri spiritual limitations
don't even try it, human science can't properly calculate it
you don't possess the amount of necessary vibration needed in order to escape it
trust me you'd be much better off staying inside that matrix
cause the point of no return is a one way destination
and word to Precise Science "everybody's not going to make it"
if I prescribed you the proper pill you wouldn't even want to take it

while the eyelids of half human reptilian hybrids continue to shape-shift right in front of our faces
you see these alien bloodlines are ancient
going back to pre-history when Draconians first infiltrated the human races
with DNA replacements and downgraded our vibration
and gradually gave your natural organic divinity a synthetic replacement
got us looking to the sky for Gods in spaceships
disconnected from the true creator while masons plagiarize Kemetic foundations
you see your third eye's been deactivated for ages
so when I tell you the truth your natural reaction is to assume that I'm hating
so like I said you would probably be better off if you just kept yo happy black ass inside that matrix

while the elite drink human blood like tonic in demonic ceremonies in order to maintain their illusionary humanity, see these
are no V's they've been here for centuries
and Obama is just the latest deception of a perception
founded in the conception of reptilian supremacy
their illest weapon yet
a melanated illuminist mason with a silver tongue that speaks a doubly opinionated
contradicted masterfully invented presented political language
I mean he's obviously the best they've created yet

and absolutely nothing has changed
Afghanistan, Pakistan, still more soldiers in Iraq while we continue to yap about Iran
ain't nothing changed
we still bombing the shit out of innocent indigenous citizens
while sacrificing the lives of ignorant Americans
engaging in premeditated conflicts in other lands
under the guise of liberation fighting against so called terrorism
while all the real decisions get submitted from the Vatican
so ain't nothing changed accept
that he's much better at executing the plan understand
he's the best, clearly the best yet
groomed to address and connect this divided mess in these times of national neglect
and public unrest in the mist of economic stress
he's clearly the best to rep
with the swagger of a Kennedy, optimism of King and some even say the smile of Malcolm X
hmmmmmmmm…
so what's next?

another stimulated package enacted to impact the nation's lack of wealth
or perhaps a new plan for your health…
well I do know one thing if nothing else
before it's all said and done
you better find yourself

Get Free!

Obama-Nation Part 3 ("the X's and O's of an enigma")

If Frederick Douglass was alive today
he would piss in Obama's fucking cereal

If Harriet Tubman was here she would smack the taste of complacency and oppression out of Michelle Obama's mouth and replace it with a shotgun... Don't oppression taste good my nigga?
Yeaaaaaaaaaaaaaaaaaaaaaaaaaaaaaah

Black Jesus is back bitch Here to heal the sick
My people's perception infected by politrix so we sip ignorance like liquors missing the bigger picture pissing out dreams and swallow polluted scriptures ejaculated by lizards out of Lucifer's platinum coded dick... yea I'm going in!!!! Obama…. OBAMA….OBAAAAAAAAAAAAAAAAAAMAAAAAAAAAAAAAAAAAAAA…

Say you had a daughter who's dating 2 dudes right, one who ain't shit and another who talk Slick but abuses her regularly and you can see the evident scars drawn across her skin tone like reverse reparations. Would you still approve the nigga who would choose to abuse your legacy and co-sign his option for maturation? Yea but niggez think I'm hating, I know you think I'm hating, welcome back, welcome home, welcome 2 Obama-Nation! I'm saying if you wanted to vote for the winner than by all means be glad that you voted for the nigga. Voted for your children sipping elixirs of desperation like fresh moscato squeezed by demons from the exegesis of a reptilian thesis, by all means vote please I mean niggez believe that he's Jesus plus he got a black wife with a big booty that's banging

Bush left the bullshit warmongers bumbling he's just picking up the pieces and keeping Israel eating besides, Obama got Osama. Free health care coming up the rare Poet peeping my people through the peephole of they souls it's cold and they sleeping

Now let's creep and seep into the deepness I carve bars in the quasars so that you can see the macro magnetize the Meta poets better get better at connecting that micro-phone to the micro match my meditation with musical tones in the cosmos and cross fade into the truth. Break the matrix code in the booth. Verses slay vipers vampires retire spit fire, transform the room into a vestibule

Lyrics inherit the mirage of spirits coming through

I'm Nikola Tesla with a text that ill test ya Wordsmith wiccans and witches with writtens riding brooms

While politicians pimp your interest
Smack the system like thick sistas on the ass and walk on stage wearing a mask like MF Doom

Now let's debate the fake vs. the truth
Political dialect that sound correct vs. the truth
A bullshit life disguised as paradise vs. the truth
"Your sacrifice" paraded on stages and mics at night vs. THE TRUTH Obama wins you lose Romney wins you lose Rockefeller wins, Rothschild wins, you still lose

The Vatican and Reptilians win, nigga you lose

It's already over

niggez sipping drinking half glass fulls of urine-ade thinking its kool-aid and soda, it's over

If Kwame Touré was here he'd take a nice wet dump
in Obama's lunch

Black hands soaked in African blood via a voting booth while AFRICOM prepares troops and drops nukes from drones and at "home" we ignore the living proof that gets shown just turn on the news and Jones to some pop tunes the black man is dead

R.I.P.black man, black man, REST IN PEACE murdered in his sleep like Fred Hampton while M.L.K.'s ghost is asking what happen to the peace Huey P's spirit with no hands clapping having dreams of blasting his piece

THE BLACK MAN IS DEAD NIGGA... GO TO SLEEP

Look outside your closed eyes realize
Triangle retinas materialize lies as truth
Sojourner doing back-flips in a sarcophagus
Trying to relocate her lost Truth
Steve Biko gets beaten to death
A thousand times in Nelson Mandela's nightmares
Choreographed by Oprah soaked in Jesse Jackson's tears
Poems written on nightsticks out of fear with bloody ice picks
White Jesus wearing the mask of Judah with a twitch
Stabbing Kwame Nkrumah to death with a broken Ankh
Disguised as a crucifix as Patrice Lumumba cries tears of acid
that form a passage written in Islamic sand script
that read God is dead, God is dead, Rest In Peace
black man black man the black man is dead
Obama's hands dripping red with the blood of slaves none of it his (but actually it is)
Your democracy is counterfeit
Zionist and illuminist wrote the perfect script
New age imperialism is a political porno flick
Puppet president's equivalent to bitch
While AFRICOM milks Africa's tits
and flies drones through the sky like giant dicks
clitoral capitalism equals satanic masturbation
while Obama's bombing dropping bombs like jizim on African nations
where the fuck is your God at????

Pray to your pockets nigga the black man is dead
Pray to your I phone
Pray to your laptop
Pray at the altar of health care and option-less stock
Pray to the God of Google and twitter that the madness will stop

Pray to Jesus, Moses, the God of Muhammad ask Allah
Pray to the Anunnaki, Pleiadian's, Plejaran's and Oz
Spit prayers in Yoruba, Arabic, Swahili and Akan
Pray with poems wrap your omens in gauze
ask the Dogon, ask Gomer, Oz and Dabar
they'll tell you the black man is dead because he forgot he was God!

If Marcus Garvey was here today
He'd take a shit on Obama's couch
and say yea I did it
then while it was still wet rub Michael Eric Dyson's face in it

we use to wear black face
now we just openly open our face
and toss America's salad until enough shit hits our face
for it to resemble a black face
and enslavement still has a black face

Assata Shakur mourns the death of Angela Davis's brain cells while demons in hell relegate
the Drac's guard they base
Shiva satellite screens shoot laser beams at ships in outer space while we sit and debate
until where blue state in the face about race

the wolf under the sheep's clothes
Dracula with his mouth closed

Like hanging around dope fiends we toke up and soak up
the privileges and benefits of membership
what's the point of joining the system to change it when you just end up
getting absorbed into the matrix
switching twisting forgetting your position and convictions
then wake up saying stupid shit like "Obama is a part of the black radical tradition"

It's sickening from within emulating the symbols and gradi status of occupying positions within the corporate system
pontificating prostitutes, corporate whores and politicians
invaded infiltrated by enslavement and mis-education
radicalism's mission met with disinterest and defeat
I speak with heat unsheathe a piece
Fuck your congressional rep
The most high is on set
Truth is you're either dead, asleep or highly upset
But your far too pressed, to be a part of the
Academic Industrial Complex

I'm done playing around people
We long since identified the problems identity
White supremacy

The devil is a liar, legitimately
Imperialism in the form of a melanated politician
His interest is their interest in-"order" to increase their intere$t

So if you cast a vote in ignorance with no diligence towards solving it
Than voting for Obama makes you a part of the problem, mother fucker
You're a part of the problem
Fuck out of here with that shit
You can't excuse your nonsense
Just admit
that ethically and intellectually you ain't shit
and just admit
that the black man is dead
rest in peace black man
nigga rest in peace nigga the black man is dead

how dare you claim the lesser of 2 evils as a choice that's legitimate?
then turn around and champion the more effective evil
evil is evil bitch, you shouldn't pick any of it
read the signs in the skyline nigga your whole mind is off point
and it's high time that God took the devil to court
he then assisted at helping the real leaders in turning war into a nice neat spectator sport
dead presidents printed on pretend cash
repto sapiens drinking fear filled blood and semen
from an intergalactic seismic energy flask
star clusters above you control the world below you
your entire reality is a fallacy put on blast
for the purpose of meta-physical merchants working
the tainted paintings of a cross bred pseudo creator god's task

you know... if El-Hajj Malik El-Shabazz was here
he would bend Obama over his knee
and whoop that fucking ass

word to Baba Dick Gregory
"now this is what this is really about"

High level scientific DNA treachery
Beyond merely theory
Advanced technological and psychological weaponry
Trans-human singularity
Word to Doctor V
"the more technological the direction we've taken, the less need for human participation"

See they got to replace their lack of biological divinity
Before the shift shifts mundane mater into collateral energy
An insurrection to prevent the resurrection of your bio-technical symmetry
But your minds religification

got you mentally
Not recognizing your souls surroundings like spiritual gentrification

We live in a computer programmed reality
Where human cattle feed the Chati Wholly
Both organically as well as energetically
Your food nigga, your fucking food
Beef cows and milk cows you're just food for the gods
A slop crop of peons sitting beneath the moon and stars

Your dead you're dead the black man is dead
Your body, your mind, your heart spirit
and soul is dead, the black man is dead nigga
the black man is dead, rest in peace black man
the black man is dead
entire diamond coded epidermis exploded
setting stiff rigged and weary
cold in a mortuary
the body of the God body rotten six feet deep in a cemetery
God is dead!

and instead where left with
"the X's and O's of an enigma"
woven into the souls cellular memory phome
like an insignia on pyramid walls
the mummified majestics from beneath the hieroglyphics encrypted
on Akhenaton's balls
"cross"-breeded with the crescent moon and stars
proceeded beyond the Venus cleft of Mars
cryogenically crocheted together with the X chromosome
of Malcolm and inserted into a CIA insurgent
make shift Mary Magdalene aka Stanley Ann
a cloned agent activated from the R complex
locked in cages at the back of your brain
the repto sapien highbred messiah with the bloodline of demons
off spring of Malcolm and Satan's syringed penis has come to reign
over the celestial circuitry of a complex matrix choreographed inside pictographs from beyond
who would believe it?
that they could re-program the birth of Black Jesus
and beseech him to kill God
your entire universe is a facade
dark matter exploding inside a stomach full of poisonous stars
constellations ejaculated with frustration in spite of Satan
until heaven finally cums/comes

now look into the mirror at your melanin/or lack there of
and I guarantee you'll see the sun
and ask yourself the question

where were you, the day the black man died
and all the Gods became One?

Ashe'

"Theme 4 Inglish"(Da B-Mix) "I Gotta Write"

"I gotta write, I have to write, these lines are my life"

"Go home
and write a page tonight
and let that page come out of you
then, it will be true"

so this is me right?
this is me write

what you see is what you get
stand on stages and let therapeutic phrases operate like mirrors
facing the faces of the people
you think this is entertainment
and I'm just up here regurgitating
out my soul for kicks
and that what I spit is simply for snaps and oohs
pounds and cd sales

cause sometimes, sometimes
it's hard to tell if their looking at the poet or the performer
the artist or the human
using pain like notes to music
and they say that the blues is the best way
to turn
hurt into harmony

so follow me, yea "follow me
into a solo that you can picture like a photo"
that I took of myself

the photographer captures such beautiful images of life
when reflecting light upon the energy of others
so I'm going turn towards the mirror and capture me
develop the film within my soul and place it on the opposite end of the glass

but if it's the negative that gets developed and shown
does that mean that the positive and true origins of our nature never see the light of day?
is the artist ever viewed for who they truly are
before the people change them?

so I'm telling you to see me for who I am
saw the true me in the mirror and captured the moment
a soul frozen with sharp shards of emotion
stuck inside my spirit like pieces of poems
so that when I write it's like I'm showing you my life

peep deep beneath the sloppy illegible ink and personalities

yea I'm Victor Frantz Rodgers the Second, son of the First
temper just like his
he always said "don't procrastinate and don't be like me
write something good son"
these are my "Hidden Chambers"
whose physical foundation no longer stands

Big Kitch rest in peace
209 Chambers street rest in peace

Transition

Transition like crucifixion
into what was written
book of my life and I'm just finishing
the chapters that he never started
author attempting to pen a better draft than my fathers
if he was here he'd say "Vic don't procrastinate"

but I've been afraid to write this page
the last barrier of the name, baptized in mill smoke and flames
            I use to let my pen imitate a gage, put it to my brain and fall face first off stage
                and the crowd would be so frightened yet entertained
              but failed to realize how I enjoyed the sheer poetry of the pain

like angels who fail from grace and for the first time could taste their own blood
                        and knew they were alive

                    beyond poetry in motion this is art in the flesh
                        my love and my stress
                        my worst at its best

                        and I'm searching

struggling to stay connected with myself
digging in old boxes of cassettes worn by time
the tapes tend to play backwards
and sometimes I just wish I could go backwards
like the words that play back-words
and return to a simpler time

                      we use to play stick ball in the yard and tackle football
                          on the concrete
                  rhyming around the table while somebody made a dope beat
                        I seem to keep flashing back

Yea I'm searching

searching for better reasons to write
these lines reflect life
and it's like this page is my mirror at night
so I'm searching, I said I'm searching

trying to achieve higher purpose in these verses
but sometimes when you broke the lines and the grind appear worthless
so I'm searching not always certain if I'm on the write path

when they say how you feel and I say aight
99 percent of the time lord knows I'm lying
but I just keep rocking this mask
I'm searching

searching right

yea music is life and I love the mic
but where's my wife?
I'm searching

                                            revisiting old themes it seems memories that scream
                                                   are much louder than dreams that whisper
                                          wishing I hadn't missed as much time with my youngest sister

she cried like the Power Puff girls had died
and so did I that one time I left
tried to tell her with teary eyes
"Joy don't worry I'll be back soon aight"

and let's just say if I was the sentimental type
I'd tell my sister Michelle how much her brother loves her
but even more importantly how much God loves her
because sometimes I'm not sure if she remembers

however our relationships a little deeper
than corny pretend hugs and kisses
I'd like to think that we just know
how much we mean to one another
been through the bliss as well as the hardships together
from priceless good memories and laugh attacks to nearly frozen in the coldest of winters ice cycles like splinters
shivered next to kerosene heaters beneath covers

and to my mother, my role model
if I could find a women with just half of what you possess
I'd be set for life

you are a warrior and I promise you with every breath of my life
that one day you won't have to work so hard
I remember how my friends spent more time at our house
then their own
cause it just felt like home

and I use to be happy then

                                                  sometimes I wish I could find a way back
                                     and I'm still searching trying to find my way in life

trying to find a point to college
trying to find a way to "be free" as an artist
free from money, flesh, and the planet itself
free from myself
God I'm searching

                                                         I want to find Jesus

                        not who he is or what he looks like, like I mean find Jesus
                            no I really want to find Jesus, find Jesus, I want to find Jesus
                                    I mean I actually want to find Jesus

No you don't understand
I need to find that nigga

walking through the projects gripping a tech that shoots life
re-writing dead scrolls reviving pages
back to their original stasis
before Homo-Sapiens starting reshaping them and him into their own image

before we had thee audacity to touch with filthy hands gifts that weren't ours to begin with
I actually want to find Jesus

wearing his real name standing on stage write next to me
delivering a message in the form of a poem to me like son
its going be okay

I want find Jes-us
I want to find Jes-us
I want to find Jes-us in us

I want to find him, I want to find him

sitting at my Aunt Teresa's bed side
with arms made of miracles
hugging the osteoporosis away
and what the doctors and physicians in that hospital
never knew
is that God held the true prescription
so no Satan you shall not
shake this family's faith!!!

and sometimes when I write it's like I'm bugging
and all I can see is the imperfection of what I create
but hopefully I've been able to make just enough corrections
to set a good example for my cousins
while David stays at the table drumming
and Daniel got those rhymes and poetic lines ready
said I inspired him to start writing poetry
but if only he knew how much his writing has inspired me

pray I live long enough to over-stand the wisdom
given in conversations with my grandmother
at least now I know that the lectures were a blessing

and when I die, when I die liquefy all my poems and music
and put them inside me in place of embalmed fluid
before you burry me
and then maybe heaven
won't even be necessary

cause no matter how hard I tried
I still couldn't find peace of mind
so I took a piece of my mind
and put a piece on these lines
so maybe if I piece together enough pieces
of my minds pieces
on these lines
through the pieces
of my mind that I pieced on these lines
I might be able to find a piece of my mind on these lines
and achieve peace of mind
in these lines
that I give to you

"Go home
and write a page tonight
and let that page come out of you
then, it will be true"

"because I gotta write, I have to write, these lines are my life"

GRIOT GLIMPSES

Return of the Griot

When I hear the drums its like God comes
When I hear the drums its like God has come

I am here

in the mist of gun claps and drum tracks the God has come back
After going back, traveling through forgotten history unraveling mysterious

In the beginning was me thee all
before break-beats books hooks and bars
Looped samples on mps or even Jimmy's guitar
Just djembes that banged like migraines inside cellular membranes
But when them came cellular soul became lost
In misdirection disconnected from self

We mental slaves with no map home
pseudo conscious drones
Plugged in charging life from the matrix like cellphones
So it seems that the griot has been replaced with a ring tone

So I lit a fire on the tip of my tongue with my heart as an alchemetic drum
Tonal hums in the form of ones and zeros
my emotions opened a gigantic poetic
time portal
Until I find myself in the ancient kingdom of Kush amongst a cypher of griots smoking
Kush no pads or pens invested in the blessing

Stepped into the center of the energies intensity and requested I want in
They laughed and said brother not yet for there is still much on which you must be
filled in

as the origins of my very existence were
re presented my position divinely commissioned
far before fox news Yakub and removed scriptures
we direct representatives of the supreme
so this poem can be equated with Nat Turner and Shaka Zulu crashing the Council of
Nicaea with bibles and blades held to Constantine tattooing his neck with prophetic
inscriptions from pens drenched in manganese and broken dreams

for all those who violated ancient sacred languages this is spoken reparations
primitively placed before imperialistic invasions and slave ships my cadence can
finally breathe while forcing Caucasians back across hot sands on their hands and
knees because the sons and daughters of God have been deceived and all good poetry
bleeds

so these pages are historically rearranging trans-Atlantic situations re-writing
middle passages returning Africans back-words on trips across thee Atlantic via my
stanzas middle passages

while ocean floors reverberate through coral reefs and create earthquakes that shake
the place like heavy bass laced with break-beats causing continents to re-shift and
drift back into the shape of the creator
Poetic Pangaea as Gaia gathers galaxies I summon shamans who speak directly to Dogon
deities spitting Coptic akashic hieroglyphic calligraphy written in ancient sacred
geometry

But... then that's when every griot in the cypher begin to speak to me... they said
unfortunately you can not re-write his-story but you can write your history
Because thee who is given much has a responsibility much larger than merely the sum
of one's parts for your life is your art but your people have been torn apart
Like worn women's hearts
Broken like re-opened wounds and c sectioned wombs

We are life's crack babies born free inside stolen tombs
With bloody blackened spoons shoved into our windpipes
while trying to gargle the trinity divided by seven
I am you you are me and we are God
Alone and out of money bumming for change trying to catch the last train back to
heaven

Who knew the railroad to eternity ran underground
And this verse is haunted by Harriet Tubman's ghost still trapped on earth
Writing poems on the bones of every slave she couldn't save
Knowing that spare presidential change
Can never cover the cost of reparations let alone revolution
people please don't throw pens at me
keep them and help me write a solution

concluded through convoluted retribution producing sacred music designing divine
blueprints
steady heavenly mucus looping confusion using my hearts sacred cadence as the beat-
box
beyond poetry this is Langston Hughes and Amiri Baraka meets The Boondocks
cause we still continue to consume bullshit music the same way we do chitlins and ham
hocks

so I talk like talking drums blended with turntables that spin akashic records
without labels
going back
unraveling all the ancient sacred mysterious and history from God to inequity
it's the return of the griot sent back to save his people

and when I hear the drums its like God comes
when you hear the drums know that God has come
listen to the drums, God has come and his voice shall be heard
children of the most high rejoice
for the griot
has returned

Huey Freeman's Diary

"I did battle with ignorance today and ignorance won. And I admit, I am often vexed by the state of my people, yes vexed is a good word. I mean you do what you can to help niggez, (I mean black people) and often end up asking yourself why you did anything at all, but niggez are our people and you got to love em regardless"

And honestly niggez don't want to be free, not only still "scared of revolution" but we've definitely become conveniently comfortable within the confines of complacent slavery
mentally auctioned off by malicious media manifestations of modern day menstruation and mangled assimilation cotton picking chicken George ass's wit movement limitations like Asian girls making attempts at booty shaking...
I'm losing patience fuck enslavement I'd rather starve and it gets so hard but shit please feed me schemes of revolutionary seeds cause I need to be free man
Simply label me the spoken word Catcher Freeman
"nigga you don't believe in Catcher Freeman, nigga you don't believe in Catcher Freeman"
(said 2nd time in high nasally voice)

Focused peeping through the window with the weapon like Malik El Shabazz spitting manifestations of a nu nation with Garvey's gift of gab
Perpetrate rap king-pens talking ridiculous you about as gangsta as gangstalicous bitch
"raise your fist I outo maim your wrists" cause most rap revolutionaries got as much to do with revolution through their music as the Christ **consciousness** has to do with Christmas
Winter solstice gerbils on your wish-list Greek mentors having buttsex with young boys in gymnasiums (or Penn State)
Saturnalia Kris Kringle media orgies capitalist festivus lineage celebrated government document documentation documented pagan elements
"Yeah I heard you, but it was boooooring Huey, blah blah blah gay sex blah blah blah congress"
"excuse me people I have an announcement to make
Jesus was black, Ronald Regan was the devil and the government is lying about 9/11"
well "congratulations my nigga, you can read"
(he speaks so well)

I mean ya'll sort of know me remotely through my poetry
but please don't ever act as if you actually really know me
cause when you're truly an artist you truly suffer the hardest often no fresh fruit for the harvest
My resume and experience says I'm qualified to be a dope poet, great, freaking great
But unlike most I'm brave enough to be me V.I.C. at CSU studied UAP "real poet type of true Emcee"
Got my degree in the field of fuck you I'm free
but freedom is expensive as shit believe me
Recently I was listening to my favorite Taalam Acey CD
and after the last track there's an outro of a phone conversation between him and Lamar Hill that shook me to my very being emotionally where Mr. Acey mentions the often stated ideology
of "it takes money to make money" even in poetry
so basically what I took away from that quote
is that sense I always been broke then I'm always going be broke

As I look down at my stack of loose leafs saturated in
"Troubled Refinery"
and suddenly it all seems like an omen withholding rolling in unfolded moments of explosive spit
and all I have to show for this shit is a big stack of fucking poems artistic peasant class much lower than yeomans
cause if you rich in spirit and optimism that simply means that you ain't shit inside of this capitalist social system
"I'm rich bitch" bullshit I'm poor nigga
but even Dave Chappelle refused to auction off his souls sacred shares to Baphomet's bankers in exchange for illuminated expanded house nigga status
And ya'll labeled him crazy
so then I guess I must be fucking nuts

but what are you to expect to reprimand or expand from a people on the stance of taking a stand who don't even understand that their standing in quicksand
You might be rich bitch with chains on your hands and yea I'm poor nigga but at least I can stand
Because I over-stand
But "what do you do when you've done everything that you know to do yet everything that you've done hasn't done any damn good? "you do what you can, Huey, you do what you can!"

But I am just a man still trying to recover the rumbling rubbage of who I am 777 degrees of the great I am divinely in cased inside organic functions of water and land from poetic stanzas composed in the deepest darkest catacombs of disregarded slave dungeons in order to discover God's plan but fucking niggers don't understand

Instead you eat chicken fuck bitches become Christians and stick your dick in the devils chitlins
while Nicki Minaj's pussy lips have sexcessfully psychologically kissed hickies of hopelessness onto the **consciousness** of young black sistas
resembling the next Pinky, Kapri Styles or Mia Mason in training
We need to revalue the values of the situation for why the black population has become the latest demonstration of blaxploitation creatively syncopated with spoken revolutionary imitations
But instead you'd rather run on stage and shout about how I'm hating on tomorrow
or scurry through the audience like Ainsley Burrows
in an attempt to convince the sheeple
not to listen or pay attention to the nutrition they were just given
poets consistently spitting spoken soul food
cause god dammit niggez sure do love the taste of ignorance

"and doom comes like a vacuum
Cause death sucks and smells like a raccoon
Or a baboon

and death kills us like crack did Pookie

like the Terminator killed Tookie
Chewbacca was a Wookie
Revolution"

I mean really, really
niggez really thought that Obizzy (Obama)
was going paint the white house black
I tell you

"it's like going to heaven and finding God smoking crack"

shit you want to talk about elevation well then try trading places with Slangston on election night placing the final touches on Obama-Nation
Ancient allegorical artistic archetypes from a bunch of creative cave dwellers carving hollow poetry like egotistic graffiti on walls in the shape of they own shadows convincing themselves that its liberation
But your 40 acres and your freedom is a figment of your own imagination soul castration cause you keep confusing amputation with emancipation
cut off from the creator when you created civilization trapped in hells favorite nation brake dancing in the basement colon filled with filthy foundations from separate but equal elixirs mixed with liquid desegregation sipping half and half's made from hatred cause somehow you've become
half slave half patriot eating chicken boxes seasoned in degradation
Bunch of Uncle Ruckus ass ma fucker's with reverse-viga-ignorance trying my dam patience

"what the hell is wrong with you people, every famous nigga that gets arrested is not Nelson Mandela
What happen to standards what happen to bare minimums?
And it's cool to love niggez but if you really love niggez so much than get niggez some help
But don't pretend like niggez are heroes
And stop the damn dancing, act like you got some god damn sense people, damn
I'm through playing around here"

"I'm retired"

"What's the point of talking, if nobody ever learns"

Sincerely,
Huey Freeman aka Slangston Hughes

Free-dumb (Complacent Slavery)

```
"I freed thousands of slaves. I could have freed thousands more, if
           they had known they were slaves."
           - Harriet Tubman
```

Everything that I say is said because I care, sincere
And everything I have and will do has been spitten and will be written
And all of its preceded meanings is out of a deep-seated love
Love, for my people

Freedom… free-dom.. free-dumb… we ain't free we dumb
free to be dumb
And this shit ain't caused by white people it's the result of nigger-dumb

Lost and divided misguided children walking through death's
dark valleys
And glorified ghettos the sun blocked out by our own shadows
Basking in fear stepping across gaping cracks in poison pavement
gashes to vast to be filled by blind faith
venomous spiritual vacancy's continually nursing our every need
with the sweet taste of complacency memories naked snatched and ripped
taken away from the very titties of our identity
incubated inside the containment's of complacent slavery
minds sterilized from the vibes of 3rd eye vision
sucking simple minded sustenance in abundance from the bosom of conditioned living
and Black Embarrassment Television
licking cracked laced semen from the white diseased penis tips of Willie Lynch's descendants and you've already
swallowed and digested cause speaking life through mics and entertainment has faded into the pixilated
arrangement of a rare accusation
like twitch, twitch, twitch…
"just mind your business, just mind your business"
Twitch

Crack babies are ice-skating on the frozen frustrated landscapes of cold castrated tongues
cause black masons, preachers and agenda given money driven
slum leeches disguised as local politicians who refuse to speak
the truth would be better off without one

freedom, free-dom, free-dumb
we are complacent slaves hypnotized by the pendulum swing of American dreams easily appeased by money and
fickle fiscal fame
a deranged existence deceased while living
inside giant block sized graves modern day slaves
pop it, lock it, drop it like black unemployment rates
with no option share cropping on minimum wage whipped and sticked in chains
now we park whips in front of project complexes and flex in platinum chains
mental shackles wrapped around the brain insane

but when I put my pen to page it all sounds so fucking lame
wordplay is played like high top fades
but whether it's crack or rap that you slang it's all the same
tossed on the cross crucified at the cost of a lost generation
and neither grandma nor Jesus can save them

and we will probably not make it
slaving in the workplace to save face for payments so that BG&E
don't turn your place into a damn plantation no you have not made it
and if Assata ain't pardoned then ain't nobody made it

free-dumb… we shall over-come
nigga its already over Obama has come…
and that nigga done
while your black card has been Trumped

free-dumb
free-dumb… nigga you are free to be dumb… as shit
talking out your ass holding a 2016 election ballot filled out on toilet paper
too complacent to wipe away your own ignorance wallowing in fecal filled self-satisfaction
we have got to be the saddest mother fuckers on the planet
and poetry's pretend purpose as the pa-late of the people has been permed to a perfection
like infinity lessons with no conception anti artistic progression
so my awareness is my weapon
so yea nod year head snap your fingers say "I know that's correct"
but all you'll probably hear when you hear this
is diatribes of doggara and dented dialect drenched in dictionary defiance
wondering why the fuck does he keep rhyming
didn't he get to the point yet?

I cried when I wrote this poem because I didn't want it to be real
But unlike photographic stills and film life cannot be correctly edited with a program
and we have been effectively programmed erased re-edited and re-programmed
just because you've become accustomed to the smell of chitlins in your grandmothers kitchen on thanksgiving
doesn't mean that your senses aren't affected by the vicious symptoms brainwashed and conditioned complacent
slaves free to be dumb within our cotton picking conditions

it's as if the ghost of Huey P. Newton is producing communal impotence while $aleing drugs to infants soul setting
on dubs big Willie Lynching
sure you can talk about freedom and fight for equal rights
but only under certain conditions
Politicians popping off policies are obviously pretenders but every single leader we have been given has been
attached to an appendix of amendments and agendas
and they the biggest boss we then seen thus far to this very day
so there really isn't any difference between Freeway Ricky Ross and M.L.K.
It's all about conditions

forget this fucking ridiculous niggez got me twitching
trigger finger itching ripping up all my black history books
in Fing effigy while I'm spitting
because Rosa's black ass had a seat
King woke up and got shot back to sleep
then Obama gave a speech

and that's it, ain't nobody been to no fucking mountain tops yet
nigga Malcolm X's grandson lived in the projects

I was probably supposed to write this like 8 years ago but
ma fuckers wasn't ready yet
Beyond dick riding you was gargling kool-aid flavored semen from Barack's nut sack spitting out hope
and yea I saw Sasha and Malia with Michelle
following big daddy O on the go and it was oh so cute
but word to Umar Bin "that shit was a real bad tv show"
nigga I ain't instigating just for the sake of historic entertainment or parading
fake euphoric race relations this is unadulterated truth propagated through the mic
you think this ish is rebellious ma fuckers I have not yet begin to write!

The bastard babies of Elijah Muhammad pop locking inside of Medusa's womb
while she vomits Ebonics
rocking trend setting poisonous snakes as locks
laced with cess, sex and death smoking chronic
mind, body and soul all woven into the mess
because everything has been compromised and everything has been contaminated
all in the name of freedom even if it means death
and I confess I can feel the stress on my chest when Nuwaubian Garvey-ite presidents
are flashing Illuminati signals in my face while I'm spitting at protests
Freedom…

Got me plunging through the septic of congested Johns feeling like less than a Legend looking for The Roots
that were infected suggesting that you should "Wake Up!"
Only to open your eyes and realize that you're still trapped inside of a second dream

the truth posted in plain sight on the facebook walls of your life and you won't even read it
illogical technological optimism presented in the form of gentri-fried chicken
and we love to eat it but believe it when I tell you that the revolution will not be twitted
and you have openly received it
the ultimate achievement of freedom

free-dumb… you have free-dumb…
and it just isn't right

James David Manning said that no one has ever made a better slave than black people
in the history of this planet and God Dammit he's right!
You have freedom… free-dom… free-dumb…
You are free to be dumb… nigga you ain't fucking free you dumb
Free-dumb… FREEEEEE-DUUUUUUUUUUMB

"If you ever find
yourself, somewhere
lost and surrounded
by enemies
who won't let you
speak in your own language
who destroy your statutes
& instruments, who ban
your omm bomm ba boom
then you are in trouble

deep deep
trouble

humph!

probably take you several hundred years
to get
out!"

and the time has come

FREEDOM!!!!!!!

Yakub

I am the rhyme that reason forgot

the time inside of time running out of time

rearranging times plot

Your malinated molested watermelon mind

Turning niggez into negros than back into niggers

suns stars moons radiant rainbows and holy horoscopes

For all my niggas

And I write poetry as if my skin is peeling off with each word
While pronouncing the whole word
Middle America depression suppressed in between the binding of my $5 chapbook
Hoping to score at least one ten in the next slam that I enter
Proving that my pain is more potent than the other poets with pain and poems pretending to be poets
Just like me

And I yes I I'm the crack laced inner city stanzas spitting faster than HipHop influenced poetic break-beats on city streets with pseudo psychological shots pop locking beats dropping as the bass keeps bumping flows fluctuating at speeds to keep the audience and the judges from finding out that I'm actually fronting

Angels entangled in the strings of devilish puppetry Gods and angels and God is a devilish angel spitting stanzas upon stanzas of poetry
With just enough saliva caught in my throat to convey
What sounds like genuine emotion
That actually says nothing

Maybe that's why it's not all that memorable
But I can make just the word Iiiiiiiiiiiiiii expand into
multiple syllables

Cause when I spit its intense even when the writing ain't shit
And I've come to preach poetry from my own personal liquor filled pulpit

And you'll be forced to listen as long as every line that I'm spitting sounds exactly like this
And I go haarrrrd as shit, even if the poem is wack as shit

And girl
I'm going fuck you so hard
That you won't even be able to fill the pain of slaves flowing through your veins
Lick upon your clitoris like wet liquorish until you begin to spew liquids from the waters of lake Kalamazoo
And the Jericho walls surrounding your G spot will then drop the same way your panties do
Right after you leave the venue
with that dude sitting right next to you

Or or oratory orbs floating in energy
esoteric revolutionary lyrical synergy
So that when I'm spitting you better listen as I rip it like this
So that just maybe they'll all remember me and my verses like church hymns
Wait wait let me think of some famous black names to say
 in between
my wordplay even if I don't know anything about them

I'm I'm I'm 4 square
4 square 7 years, 4 square and 7 years
Inside 4 squares, 4 square and 7 years
4 square in between here and there
But going nowhere, flying in Nike airs
Believe it, hustle so hard I could sale a paraplegic
A flight of new stairs, and you don't want no warfare
Dopest poet to open the opus floating setting like lotus
So focused so focused I'm watching you watch me
Watching your girl watch me God watching my watch
Watching me watching my watch and its time
For the audience to notice me
So now what do we notice

Hmmmmmm…

now do any of these styles sound familiar

Spoken word cloning cum coated
Yakub poetry
cause poets been grafting they whole style and persona
from other poets
diet dopeness… dooping the audience into thinking that what you spitting is the truth
but what you spitting isn't you
honestly ya'll metaphors and similes need to be on Maury
cause the father of your style is someone other than you

unenlightened biters discussed as entertaining writers reciting
in the image of another niggez lyrical likeness
but nothing you approach the mic with
was ignited in your own voice
cause you don't have one
yet as soon as you step on stage all of a sudden you got a different voice
huh?

how the fuck you got a poetry voice???

Hey Yo spoken word has become token word and word
these art-aficiul ass wordsmiths
need extensive help
maybe you'd be a better poet if instead of trying so hard to be a poet you focused on being yourself

but it all just seems useless
lackluster lyricists looking stupid steady Yakubing
beyond paragraphs you then even graphted pre-choreographed theatric stage movements
a little bit of this and that and of course a couple of these

shaking your hand faking emotional sincerity imitating Taalam Acey
but lack the actual skill or profound writing
speaking while seeking reaching your hand into your pocket
for Lamar Hill's stolen style so you can recite it
pausing your set to sip from plastic poetic bottles filled with liquid A.T.M. wordplay sucking up all the Archie but left behind
the entire message

come on son
I can see the difference between imitation and innovation
cause you're spitting a cloned cadence that's uncreative making poetry resemble a recycled record same song continually spinning to no end
somebody needs to break the cycle with a pen

cause honestly most of these hosers posing
as the next Poet Emcee's is just Yung B
body language all boisterous
Poets too Def to hear anything other than the inflection
of their own Slave New Voices projected on the TV screen
unable to see any history prior to 2003 open your mind
word to Eli "the revolution has been compromised"

nigga please
if you "Langston Hughes on steroids"
then I'm obviously Amiri Baraka meets Bruce Lee

see you going have to go back a whole lot further to find me
to Gylan Kain on top of the roof top
or maybe perhaps a prophet from Watts
heavy weighted words woven into the concrete
or maybe if you could manage to find
You Tube footage of a Fredrick Douglass speech

cause evidently it seems that the spoken word art as a practice has become just acting and reenacting vocally stepping to the m.i.c. with Yakub poetry
cause your whole style is grafted from somebody else's nuts
so how about you innovate and originate for once and actually step your writing up
yea I said it

now what???

Why Does The Woolly Mammoth Howl At Midnight???

The moon looks like Harriet Tubman's third eye

blinking

Sitting on top of Africa's bosom tittys talking in

tornado tongues

To a def platypus spewing putrid poems into the abyss

of midnight

My mangled mamas mulatto melanin makes Martha

Washington wonder where the years went

While the sun is still laughing looking into the

lake

Lama limbs licking up more metaphors on your

tongue for you to taste

Poet your pen holds your purpose, so what you

wield should be worth it

Let not your words ring worthless

Stories tossed into the wind like smoke signals

that only form formless clouds of poetic pollution

Pseudo dope quotes that hold hollow solutions

Yo so called sacred scriptures are about as divine

as a Madea storyline because sometimes...

the boisterous buffalo bellows bereavement on the

borderline of madness

Black Jesus singing lullabies to Malcolm X's ghost

riding a stuuuuuuuuttering stegosaurus through Harlem

Calling on slave songs broken notes dipped into an

old ladies esophagus holy black Baptist soup Batman

Obama's grandmamma cooking and choking on heavenly

hymns in Sudan, ma fuckers you knowwhatimsayin

Standing on stage with the world's ear lobes

lingering at your finger tips and no more to offer the audience

other than metaphors drenched in frivolously placed "paper

clips" cause you aint saying shit

Moving through stanzas searching the surface for

clues to where the meaning behind all the ohhs went

Poetic devices and writing tools misused to the

extent of bastardazation

over theatric antics that you dare mislabel as personification

but didn't add any human like qualities to a non-human

object

creative writing 101 bitch, a play with whack

wordplay and no poetic aesthetics is not personification

you can't just call stuff stuff and think it's

going be that stuff because you called it that stuff... eaghhhhhhhh

enough

and everyone is to afraid to tell you the truth

about your metaphoric abuse and it's not right

and what you write disgusts me like

pregnant mothers sucking down nicotine and

spitting up profanity on a block in park heights
(now that was metaphorical)

I remember when my mother baked bread

on Santa Claus' back

lifting lilacs to the sun like

Ikarus wax wings on a lonely deranged duck who doesn't

like crust on Tuesdays

Slaves died for this and Martin Luther King probably

cried for this

serenading my hands to the stars like babies

drinking similac soaked in hope

A white pelican with no rhythm moon walking across

Michael Jackson's skeleton

Stanzas written in hieroglyphic jism so that my prophecies

could come first

Listen to the drums in the distance yelling like a

pomegranate on coke trying to cope

With the hollow dreams of plastic fruit
we are all

lost mangos with no juice

Scratching are inhibitions like dry chicken on Easter

Like the eyeballs of an elephant with alzheimer's receiving
confessions inside of a bathroom

That overheats from hot shit, prehistoric orthodox
animal priests

That rises to the peak like inner city deadbeats

filled with turpentine and yeast

As the devil begins to flinch searching on google

for your forgotten innocence

Like like like like an exploding armadillo assulted

by an angry walrus

Living inside a poem about a poem inspired by

a poem that has nothing to do with the poem

Even tho it was quoted in the past tense

So many animals I mean metaphors in my poem and none of them make

any sense

If the points don't matter then why isn't every

poem perfect?

I refuse to except that every piece is worth

at least a 9.5 or higher that gets spit

If that was fact than crap like this wouldn't exist

sterile lyrical content

Rhymes on top of rhymes inside lines combined with
over romanticized wordplay

More metaphors mushed into your poem than homo-sapiens
pushed into a New York subway
in the middle of a weekday

Illusionary recitings that seem highly exciting
dressed up on stage disguised as good writing

Slam coaches constantly co-signing

Thundering applause in the form of an art form dying

Obi-Wan vs Darth Sidious
and your too ignorent
to realize where the lines are dividing

Poetically paralyzing, creative complacency no
growth in the recipe imitation and infancy

You are crawling not climbing through stagnant
stanzas that barely breathe

A whole "heard" of woolly mammoths ramming through

spoken words future before it's even conceived

Now I'm far from an elitist slinging dogma drama

like lyrical leaflets

But I swear if I hear one more meaningless mammoth

sized metaphor I'm going rip off my beard and freaking eat it

Shouting soliloquies from the rooftops of Shamballah

carrying basins filled with lost memories

Extracted out of Marcus Gravy's mental synopsis

Noble Drew Ali instrumental rapping

Sojourner Truth juice mixed with Harriet Tubman

corn nuts, I can jump to the moon in my air Haile Selassie's

And dunk on Saturn's rings if "Yakub" trys to watch me

on an odyssey in an invisible city

Sucking sustenance from the perforated organic bosom

of a Tubman titty

Babbling in kool-laid flavored similes like a

confused child on a train listening to a deranged crab

In the form of an old lady preaching backword theologies

as she dances naked beneath the moon in broad daylight

We are the children of fallen angels with wings

made from lactating mothers covered in intergalactic pie crust
WHAAAAAAAAT!!!!!!!!!!!!!!!!!!!!

You see because the woolly mammoth is really a man-myth

for man's myth with the mammoth for a man's myth

or man's width from man tits that milks the man-widths
man-myth until
it becomes
MAMMOTH!!!!!!!!!!

And see you probably just thought that all of this

was real, you probably actually bought into all the bullshit

And mangled molested metaphoric madness that don't

mean shit, and you bought into it

At some point you actually believed it and

probably snapped and clapped

You actually whole heartedly believed in it

Like remixed religious texts shoved down the necks

of catholic parishioners pasted to the pews by pedophile priests

Ejaculating poisonous scriptures down their throats

Steady digesting Satan infesting infecting your intestines

And the truth is hard to swallow, harder than

hardships and life lessons wrapped inside blessings

So I ask thee, just two questions…

Wordsmith why waste words when you write?

And why oh why does the woolly mammoth howl at midnight?
Eoooooooooooooooooooowwwwwwwwwwwwwwwwwwwww

"Words Don't Die"

You know you really got to watch what you say
Like tantrum tangled tongues dipped into frustrated fung-swayed film clips and digital photos spoken spitting into existence like Nommo no you really got to watch what you say
Because words live
Every verse vivid visions vocalized birthed out of minds divine sequels
Words are more alive than most people
Poetry energy every piece you speak potentially lethal
Words are alive

visual lyrical spiritual paintings and the children are watching like little future versions of you in training untangling deception every child facing the clouds searching for blessings seeking protection in your lesson plans and hope always seems so topical but faith is not optional because teachers are like powerless creatures facing gigantic frantic obstacles

I wonder at what point does the boundless joy and triumph in a child's eyes suddenly transform into standardized sorrow
I think the pointless politicians and bureaucrats doing crap in they offices need to be tested for incompetence
And schools don't have God or bibles so it always feels like I'm fighting a war with paper bullets and plastic rifles cock back my tongue "beats, rhymes and life" every night I write the sun

Cause this poem is for Dana (Teon) Danny, Dane' Diamond, James, James, Joseph, Jeremy, Josiah, Jamie, Joy, Jeffery, Jasmine, Janae and Justin, Isis, Tre, Raheem, Bradford, Shihyem, Myisha, Malcolm, Marcus, Mara, Megan, Mykira, Mihija, Myiera, Nieja, Nashei, M.J., Brion, Briauna, Bruce, Bridgette, Brandy, Bishop and Dontae

They are in every line these words are alive living my mission depictions proficient infinite endless pictures written into imagery symmetrical geometrical symmetry content as creative as
Kemet's Khemestry vocally vibrates
Until we grow up and can't recollect correct how to connect and activate our soul's sacred alchemy

Born artists incarnated to embark upon our destiny's we are heavenly majestic yet skeptic held captive by life's complications so childhoods die alongside imaginations "Waiting for Superman" to land standing on a stack of budget cuts and late legislation urban populations mis-educated by state ordered stipulations operated from oppressions latest equation but oh no they don't
"know how to act" it's their fault, these children are problems they cause issues but personally most of my problems and issues
are with the adults

it makes me sick, higher ups sip our tears from silver spoons and make their plate off the strength of our ignorance continuous emancipated pages of desegregated bliss makes neither dollars nor sense
enacted inaccurate business practices tactics drenched in filthy factions of
white people shit
but they don't want to hear it because parents, politicians and principals can't handle the truth
no Alonzo I don't work for you I Am employed by the youth
which must just mean nathan ever since O'Malley effectively cut

96 million from the state's budget for education while faculties have meetings inside inferior facilities about the next meeting where they prepare for another meeting and have a meeting and set the agenda for the meeting after the following proceeding meetings leading to another meeting where they take notes on the previous meeting and have a meeting about the meeting and the cycle keeps repeating we need to start eating our ideas and begin producing solutions like music
spoken into movements one of my students said
"poetry is the light the sun uses"

so I wrote this for Ariel, Area, Antonia, Arlette, Ashe, Sha, Amanda, Ashley, Amene, Anthony, Anthony, Amean, Armand, Alexis, Alexis and Amara, Laquan, Taquan, La'Tashia, Harvey, Hannah, Unique, Tyrique, Thomas, Tawanda, Terry, Tyshon and Unika, Kierra, Khadijah, Quentin, Chauncey, Corey, Corey, Courtney, Candice, Chardonnay and Wendy

and even though I've already seen her vision and know that her name is Rhythm heaven forbid I should have children in the midst of this existence cause the teacher me and the artist me each have equal expenses
and I always try to give change to the homeless yet knowing that if things don't change I remain only one inch of a bad decision away from where their sitting

potent pain producing profound poems and every day the struggle stays so intense because yes "money matters" but when it comes to what matters most I am rich
more than a myriad of married meanings metaphors are like Mujaheed when I write I'm just trying to "fight the good fight" with my pen

so to every child with the God given spark of art every future fire spitter torchbearer I've had the privilege to reach and connect with
because you never really teach until each student
becomes someone you can learn from
and they taught me how to lyrically harness the power of the sun

so I spit this for Foster, Fantasia, Ebony, Kahlil, Krae, Veronica, Asia, Deajae, Deon, Darius, Daniel, Deniero, Deiondre, Derrick and Dizzy for Phillip, Nehemiah, Sunshine, Larry, Lavandel, Lemell, Sha, Kweosha, Sharde, Shaquille, Christian, Coco, Rani, Chris, Tavon, Thomas, Tierra, Sue, Melvin, Michael, Mecca, Mariah, Morgan and Mia, Nikki and Nakia

Words live internal external visual immortal imagery lyrical legacies poetry power "Joy's Pudding" eternal energy

And to Corey Barnes no longer with us physically your writing inspired me
more than you ever had the chance to know
only 12 years old
mic check i can still see him standing on top of that desk shutting down the show
and somehow a moment of silence just seems so inappropriate
because yet even though this flesh is merely temporary

WORDS DO NOT DIE

AND NEITHER WILL OUR FUTURE!!!!

X-Men

It's like we're the X-Men

And Daniel is Wolverine

Skelton like emotions coded with adamantium as swag

Liquid stanzas dancing like a warrior's song inside his heart beat

And if he doesn't speak what's on his mind he might burst

Truth spoken poems woven into his spine like surgical procedures

But like a true leader he always puts his team first

And Lemell is definitely Nightcrawler never really present but always present

At the very second you need him most

Skinny yet possess a will stronger than sulfuric acid burning through hardships

A poets tongue shoved between a preachers lips

Pieces composed of prayers pent together in his finger tips

Shadow boxing with God's favor

And Christian… Rogue a marvel waiting to explode from inside

Uncertainty ticking like a nuclear bomb beneath the calm in her vocal chords

Poems punching out the animals of self-doubt fleeing from her spirit

Trying to fight back tears with the strength of tsunami memories

And she'll be able to fly one day

Just from the touch of destiny's skin absorbing truth

Confidence cascading a quiet constellation caught in Gods cornea

X-Men

And Rani… now that's Psylocke

One person 2 body's cervix inertias fighting like the
moon vs. the sun

De-mens lying like devils crying and she is just trying to become one

With herself

Pen slicing like schizophrenic psychic blades across a lonely notebook page

While the truth runs like Christ out of an empty grave

My daughter from Shamballah our minds the same

half poet half insane

Troubled waters doused in heavens flames natural beauty' embedded in her brain

While Lola's like a lyrical liaison words dancing on the tip of her tongue

But I am so proud of who they both will become

Hey yo son dat dude Armand, Cyclops

Ambitions blended with sharp lyricism locked in on fate

Potent paragraphs like seismic blasts

A solar flare crashing into midnight

Powered on the inside by concealed feelings

Covered with the prophetic habits of rose colored glasses

So you can never really stare behind the stanzas

In scripted on the surface of eyelid intentions

On stage next to Nikki aka Jean Gray

Pulling the polluted princess from out of a queens DNA

Fueled by competitive flames

Creative fire tide rising like a Phoenix from the page

Transcending freedom on the wings of salvation erasing uncertainty

Until the scores no longer matter

While every line from her mind splits matter

Stanzas like a telekinetic dancer

My nigga Shaq

Dats Gambit da gambler sly ass pimp diva

La Bella Prince finger prints heating up poetic pamphlets for protest

Freeing the dumb until freedom is their only process

Master at shuffling life's madness like a card deck

Snatching victory from the clutches of impossible

Regardless of the unfair hand he was dealt

Now Nakia, that's Storm

Ensence the mental stimulant wordplay like a weather witch

Thesis that speak with thunder writing like lighting

True poet griot goddess with a nation of narration and Nommo woven into her lisp

We are X-Men

Now get this, Melvin... dat nigga is Bishop

Verbally injected his verses with a virus sick

With Uncanny wit, ahead of his time

Like he traveled back in time with futuristic rhymes to spit

The ability to absorb life's negativity transmitted into creative energy

And fired back with intensity into the face of the bullshit

Vocals ripping vivid imagery with ghosts inside his cadence

In the form of secret agents downloading rhyme schemes

Wordplay that plays like bootleg movies on wide screens

Taylor... Mystique, deep, unique

Emotional shap-shifter, flipping drifting shifting

Love into enlightenment with a smile bigger than her excitement

Standing in front of a mic about to rip

Tierra is shadow cat, because she disappeared

After I pushed her too hard through a wall of her own apathy

I'm sorry

I'm telling you we're the X-Men

Thomas is Iceman

He's on the team wait he's not

Oh he's back now? He isn't?

Feelings covered by a cold too frigged for faith to witness

Coco you know that's Jubilee

Poetic inspiration in the form of sparks

Shooting from her finger tips like "testimonies"

Setting the listener free

And Alison, she's obviously Emma Frost, the White Queen

Not always quite clear if she can be on the team

Compositions frozen mental fire spoken inspired motions floating

Metaphors molding meaning from mystery

See we are not poets we are X-Men

And Olu is Princess Lilandra naturally

Poet from another planet imaginatively

Dashing through galaxies

Mother landing the mother-ship

Nourishment and leadership provided in abundance

Now Kenneth, my nemesis Professor X the best

Actually practices what he poets like mantras

Telepath paragraphs that lift mind-states out of depression

Inspiring future leaders once lost

Cerebral maps etched by life's lessons

From children split like atoms

Who fought monsters mentally mangled

by the mutations of adolescence

Pieces that lift injured spirits like a telekinetic stretcher

Trying with just drive and a message to make an entire community rise

Like prostitutes off of knees when a job is finally finished

Resources reneged upon budgets ripped by recession

Cause trying to save the world with poetic lines and purpose that's divine

Is like trying to stand straight with a shattered spine vertebrate victimized
by city council lies, or win a political foot race while paralyzed poems pounding pavement
With no trace of where the inflection changes like pages without lines

And I'm, well me, I am Magneto

A villain who wants to believe he can be the hero

And I am willing to bring this pitiful place to its hateful knees

Like a happy hooker if it means saving my people

Poets… or rather mutants with unusual inhuman powers on microphones

A poetic leap forward in artistry's evolution

Inspiration locked in our DNA codes ready to explode like smashed atoms

Because coaching a team of young poets is like leading a league of mutants into Genosha

Limitless liquid dimensions cosmic creative energy looping at light speed inside of God's circular system

Listen I am a freaking mutant and mics are made of metal making my emotions magnetize meaning Magneto

And it seems like pain is what I attract the most

And this electro-mic-netic force field composed of poems

Won't protect me from my reality

But maybe if I pull purpose and good people in my direction

The intensity of this magnetized inspiration can positively affect them

Cause I'm a bit vicious spewing verbal venom with my villainous ways

But I promise you my intentions are as righteous as white kids

Rocking Che Guevara shirts with no idea who he is

Magnetic mind manipulation and just maybe I can reverse the polarity of this magnetized energy

If I pull enough love out of the people surrounding me

Metamecha metallics the inertia pull of gravity inside of our chest cavity

The philosophers stone rhythm of your heart beaten into a shattered jewel

There are precious metals inside all of you

And I am not a poet, I am an alchemist

Stare into your soul's entrance and tell you the truth

It's not worth it don't pursue this

As useless as Eunuch's a naked savior dancing to the muted music of purpose

Go get a freaking job, wield your words on weekends

This poetic preaching is worthless

Don't pick up a pen it I'll make you a mutant… an X

Men

And you already know

That we don't play super heroes

We are super heroes

We are X-Men

SLANGSTON X

I wonder if Spike Lee has cointel papers as wallpaper outlining the insides of his house

What if Denzel Washington was closer to George Washington

embarking marching a generation of neo intellectual plantation slave agents across the waves of poison processed Potomac
hair follicles
astrological philosophical debacles

What if Linwood X was Judas bumping futuristic rap music

hand in yo pocket using the movement's
very blueprints like rifles

aimed at Christ's most promising disciple

no more than icing on the cake of history's fakest debates

so when I write slice mics like a
wordsmith wolverine

X genes encoded in my rhyme schemes

faiths fallacy I am fate the future laced in my palms

spirit of the honorable Elijah Muhammad tossing knowledge at your face

but your tongue is too numb to the taste to speak anything opposite

of the hate created by hate

it seems we often have a hard time seeing the humanity in our hero's

we are all filthy field Negros picking at
one anothers insecurity's

like cotton in the sun
chained to our own beliefs

so we speak what we know not and believe whatever were told to think

drowning in 2nd hand biographical ink

while information changes more hands then coke deals

but deeper still much deeper still

the truth has been permed to the root since youth

spiritually stripped of its nutrients like black hair

Medea molesting Madam CJ Walker walking through your nightmares

tap dancing on split ends for ends baptizing your mind

in vicious Christian dogma and yellow 5
got you running with closed eyes Americanized trying to wash away your own thoughts like hot relaxers

cause if knowledge and wisdom was rhythm you'd probably drop the beat like hungry rappers and start snitching to master

but what less would you expect from devils in the flesh

spit the truth with my dying breath
Slangston X

slice out my tongue and drop the message
on your front steps

Central intelligence agencies and federal bureaus of investigated bureaucracy pulling plagiarized Isis pages out the pentagon's basement co-signed by Arab masons

the bastard child of orthodox Islam and Lucifer

getting butt fucked by the ghost of J Edgar Hoover

No need for sharp shooters when double barrel shot guns are aimed at close range

high fiving white Jesus in the bleachers singing glory glory hallelujah

with no soul like it's regal

bullets raining down from on high like fire on your pain

Nigga fuck the government I aint never scared

but the government is scared of to many free black people

But were still too afraid to see what's true cause there is no Luv 4 Self if you hate my reflection because it looks too much like you… hmmmm

Maybe we're too late or perhaps it's too soon to assume

that professor X I'll just walk in the room

Manipulated mutated metamecha miracles
the reincarnated voices of hung slaves singing negro spirituals resonates throughout Fard Muhammad's empty tomb while the sound of Nat Turner's shot gun rounds can be heard

echoing off the walls of Malcolm X's
hollowed out bullet wounds

While his daughters shed bitter waters inside of a lonely mosque at the foot of their father's cross outside bombs are going off

Korans tossed like hand grenades in the direction of a transparent Zion

and you can hear Betty Shabazz crying streams of fire from
Sunni Muslim eyes

cause it's hard to tell truth from lies when false gods redefine holy lines

in the name of the most high

Celebrated deflated pride amputated
black fists
still trying to rise

In a racist society designed to keep its subsidized dichotomy trapped inside

the "Theology of Time", tick tick tick
all rise all rise

let the messenger's hands rise

like Mosses holding off army's beneath
Mt. Sinai at night

TOCK

Armageddon is canceled!!!

Cause we need more balance of analysis

between truthful statements and bloviated
intellectual masturbation

ejaculating with lack of fertilization on the square foundation

perhaps there's not enough "Art" and too much "Conversation"

So they'll probably try to murder me
on the mic for my rhymes

then dig me out the grave to be killed a second time

but too much truth was produced from the "grassroots" of my scribes to

"Reinvent" eternal life

If your father was a martyr
and your mother is a whore
than there just isn't

any way to ignore the fact that you're dead on the inside

I seem to sense an X gene in your president's bloodstream

Beyond the enigmatic X's and O's of sankofa sports scrimmages

so warfare gets declared between images and immigrants

while hustlers work 24/7 to feed fiends and receive no health care or benefits

ask Reagan, now that's "taxation without representation" on your decedents

so the "white news media" reacts blame it on "crime by blacks"

and 30 year old ghetto grandmothers who sip on yak while singing the blues

"police brutality" and "mob violence" choreographed by "white liberals and Jews"
confused bloody ballads of hysteria, bite the bullet and cast a ballot rather than face the challenge of "race war in America"

niggez bitching about snitching when "housing conditions in black communities" are already reminiscent of prisons

ridiculous politicians roosting chickens

ovens filled will biscuits

and it's a fact, that there can never be a "united black front"

as long as our streets are still divided by crack

now where's the "resurrection" for your spiritual relapse

Christ cast demons into swine
and turned water into wine

so I guess that makes it divine
to dine on spear ribs

and live as functional alcoholics

and you'll still find "crime inside of a gentrified Harlem"

where the black man's muse reads the news and sings the blues in front of Langston Hughes' house starving

and the headlines read like an apocholiptic drama

Miley Cyrus, Kanye and Osiris, Lady Gaga smoking ganja with the Ghost of Amy Winehouse and Osama

Justin Bieber twitters Martin Luther King's dream was cool monument built upon the scene of the crime

but Lil Wayne

had the best diamond encrusted slave chain of all time, of all time!!!!

Word to Elijah Muhammad's baby mama's minister Farrakhan strapped with a suicide bomb
in the shape of an X etched across his chest bear hugging Obama

while Castro is shitting in his pajamas haunted by the ghost of every dead Kennedy

and Manning Marable riding a "Pale Horse" named selective memory

headed for the white house under a
secret identity
screaming

FREE MY NIGGA, FREE MY NIGGA, FREE MY NIGGA MUHAMMAD

while time magazine imposes upon
Malcolm Shabazz the Second

to stand next to the window posing holding the M1 just like his grandfather

soul stolen cameras flashing like
cannons blasting
mic left smoking

no words of solidarity spoken
black helicopters dropping doctrines of
mass destruction over top of Mecca

and Harlem's lungs just exploded

and all that was left
was a poet overdosing on HOPE
holding his chest

bullet holes in his text…

I AM SLANGSTON X

The Pedagogy Of Points

"Poetry is a political act, it involves telling the truth! And in the process of telling the truth about what you feel or what you see each of us has to get in touch with him or herself in a really deep and serious way!" –June Jordan

Poems are often like people who won't look you in the eye

Like a whole truth infiltrated by half lies
Poems are mothers molding meaning holding aborted babies baked in confusion
Still born poetic children trapped in the illusion of time

And space

On lines

Writers who recite on mics with tainted tongues attempting to taste greatness
Impatient incubation illustrating creative complacency with closed eyes

The shadow of a pen on paper 2 sides both divine in their relation to connectivity and creation
No face value interpretation from expression
stressing lessens the lesson pressed into facial expressions
it's not that I don't see the blessings embedded in the process
but at some point the points should promote growth in the content!

The pedagogy of these points cannot be placed inside a pimps grading system
Miss-education missing the vision in the mission blinded by the addiction to mimicry
Faiths flames flickering in the light of hells imagery
But who are we to define poetry????

Because honestly "poems are bullshit!!!!"

Yea poems are bullshit

if there not hot bricks smoking from fire as frustration

flung at audiences forcing them to build foundations in places where faith once occupied inaction

poems are like lies disguised as revolution shooting doctrines of poison pollution like pesticide

from inside of Al Sharpton's mouth

digested in the confessions of Jesse Jackson's fecal matter laced falacio habits

cause poems ain't shit unless they can rip redundancy like rust out of rhetoric's ramblings

replacing rancid fruit with the righteousness of truth

I don't want to listen to poems written for inspiration

unless they actually agitate hollow motivation

providing blueprints for the youth

HEY POEM… FUCK YOU!!!!

Fuck you poem if every line inside of you is not exploding like suicide bombers

inside the consciousness of those once considered conscious before they casted their ballots

for an Obama-Nation when in the end all Obama did was just bomb more nations!

At the notice of novices on stage acting like prophets exploited for profit

Poetry as perjury inside of purgatory playing pageantry pretending to produce movements

Not nearly enough evolution in your writings or recitings to ignite a revolution

What's the point of your poem if you're fronting

cause if you're not saying something

when you're saying something

then you're not saying something

"we need assassin poems" leaving bullets like stanzas lodged into the cerebellum of every soulless Rothschild

and Rockefeller reptilian vampire bastard on the planet

Poems like panther teeth that eat through imperialist regimes

beating the orphaned children of Martin Luther King's dead dream

back to life

Poems with metaphors as defibrillators invading your lungs shocking hearts back into action

A piece needs more than just a piece of passion

Cause poems are death slowly stepping towards a mic

in the form of a purposeless life

unless they are light held in a child's hands nourished until its exposure exposes eternity

and every offspring or verse they recite are birthed as angels in flight at night

forcing you to reawaken and stand up

because poems should tell the TRUTH

OR SHUT THE FUCK UP!!!!

A poem plastered into the open fist

of a young Angela Davis

pimp smacking awareness back into her present day self

because to me poems are still bullshit if there not

currently currency configured masks

ripped off of presidents faces replaced with unwelcome truth

poems should easily be

the spirit of Steve Cokely

relinquished as information

exploding from within my pen

impaling pale skin Jewish men confessing fire from

Zionist lips

laced with a poison lisp hissed into hope

so poet please muster just enough pain to bleed on page then promenade across stage

in attempts to gain qualification points place and PSI rank

like truth yanked from the clutches of insanity

don't get mad at me

I am just the voice of your own reason speaking bleeding believing bringing truth back into season breathing

life back into where death once slept like dat nigga Jesus

but I guess if a kid isn't part comedian or able to cry

at command on stage

then they're not considered for the pantheon of the greatest creative writers these days

but sometimes all I seem to see is poets pimping

there pain just the same

All of we trying to see who can bleed the best off page

an artist's catharsis's for healing

when in reality

Poetry is like the health industry

sure we can all diagnose the diseases in our thesis

but it's time we started creating some cures in our pieces.

So when I spit I need this poem to hit like the vaccines for aids, diabetes and cancer

cause if

you really want the truth as an answer

they all actually exist

And I know we concoct hot rhyme schemes

stitch intense poetic scenes

and form tightly knit teams

but the biggest difference between slam and athletics

is that "poetry is never about dominance

but making a connection"

and yea I know that the points is never the point

but rather the poetry

but what's the point of having the points

if they don't produce better poetry

So please why don't you humor me

and try to score this!

Sundiata Lives!

WARNING!!!! (the truth follows below)

Your skull is like a plantation

And the follicles that grow are the people

The slaves

Engraved into their patterns like braids

And over time your mind has been fertilized to produce bullshit

And the fruit of your roots pummeled by the pesticides of propaganda and media lies

Huggggggh... let us begin

You see perms are the processed or rather the process of slavery

Relaxing the conditions or actually conditioning you to relax in your conditions

Washing what's on your brain or rather brainwashing what's on your brain

Perms permanently perming the permanence permeating your permanent condition

Haaaaaa… but I'm just bullshiting (laughter)

Cause once you're relaxed in your perm-anently enslaved state

Hair (lol) comes the conditioner of scripture to keep you straight

No need to look to the goddess she not safe

They've already strained her with a straightener

So now you straight

Announcement… too many black people vote!

What up my nigga…

(imagine how much power we would have if we stopped giving them the power, stopped asking and did)

pay attention to the mathematics of the mentally imprisoned

See it's all about division

Cause once you've been processed into submission

like prison

you now move in contradiction to your natural condition

making it easier for them to *part* the people into a particular position

cause now we split, worried about making ends

work till you can barely stand to your feet

but your doom for defeat if you work to your bitter end yet the ends still don't meet

so we try to split ends and like spliffs we split at the end

and at the end we just split, with no ends

I tell you… Jesus just might have been the worst thing to ever happen to niggez!

(if you walk into an old black ladies house and see a picture of a white Jesus on the wall, in your mind do you say hey it's white Jesus? no you just think hey it's Jesus… smh)

Alright… so you rinse and repeat, the same process of being processed

Generation after generation of genocide with more follicle homicide as the onset

Yo roots then died and been fried like HipHop and chicken

Got you a whole spread of HipHop Chicken (like they a catering company or something)

White Jesus walking across led infested troubled tap waters bleeding saintly salvation from the spigot

Ascending from a bucket of fresh chitlins griping a plate of baphomet's best bacon glistening on top of a buttered boule' biscuit

shake yo body at the party to that new illuminati bitches

now let me show you wack spitting mimics the difference

between hoetry and poetry

your writing ability has absolutely everything to do with your intellectual agility

yet your poetic content is more like politics

pseudo conscious nonsense

a bunch of non-innovative writers and closet coons

    cinema enemas pretending to be progressive with yo pen   tip

but didn't innovate shit

your stanzas sound like already chewed food when you spit

your barely Tyler Perry bitch

while I'm Patrice O' Neal with the skill

Dick Gregory with a savory rhyme scheme mixed

with Dave Chappelle's resistance

none of you poets are better at poetry than me

you're just better at promoting poetry than me

fuck this shit!

(but anyway, I digress) I guess?

the first slaves came over on a ship named Jesus

then slaves were whipped and put in chains in the name of Jesus

now you sing and make praise in the name of Jesus

now I'm not hating on that nigga Jesus

cause Jesus is that nigga

but nigga I'm just saying, you know what I'm saying nigga

I should probably just stop now right? Write?

See honestly Madam CJ Walker was a bigger king pin

Than Freeway Ricky Ross could have ever been

You could lay a whale scale in front of baal

And try to weigh the difference

Between crack rock and Chris Rock movie scripts

And niggez still wouldn't get it

It's not your hair that's bad it's your damned condition

Cause your scalp is a plantation

And the follicles that grow on the surface are the people

And just cause you got locks don't mean that you then unlocked shit

Just locked in to thinking you on some conscious shit

Cause you went from instant to incense

Bunch of illegitimate Islamic fundamentalists fumbling over their own common sense

The gods in your nation's earth leaning towards the east for peace

The Rasta in the streets with imposter beneath his speech

Niggez be more Mormon than Moorish contaminated by the beast

Giving me a Kemetic headache with the aesthetic of pseudo deep

Faking like you than awakened but beneath the plantations acres you still sleep

Yea you got locks but you still locked into one way of thinking

Why you think they called locks than?

You better un-lock something from within

I mean what's the point honestly?

Cause it seems that

HipHop is dead

And poetry is gay

Literally (oh really?)

You must be out of yo cotton picking mind

Maybe you need to watch "The Help" a few times

While setting beside someone from those times

Before the truth can actually rise

Cause there are clearly crops of cotton caught in yo mind

Too relaxed by the lye of lies to realize

Pressed until you barely alive

Trying to weave together a way to survive

Comatose by time

You better wake up or die

I bet you didn't even know

That "Frederick Douglas fights monsters that pee on people's eyes"

Now let's open wide

I'm a take you to the other side

No bullshit, far past the polatricks and drama

Word to the tender scalp on my nappy headed mama

    I'm talking aliens, Egypt and Shamballah

With just enough creamy crack in the crevasse of your naps

To snap Harriet back into the act

You deserve a pimp smack for that wack ass snatch back

Beyond conditioned so assimilated that you're dying to be a patriot of this nation

Manipulated by traditions, vicious Christian convictions

Dripping like lard from the fixings in the kitchen

The devils hot mittens flipping, sistas barely getting back in the kitchen

But you forgot barely remembering the wisdom positioned in the back of yo kitchen

Obviously it's plain to see that the poison P'S axioms of niggerdom remain a dire concern

I'm talking about pork and perms

Just observe the mess we stressed

Post traumatic slave syndrome at its best

While we still crying trying to find "change"

Yet the money changers

Is getting ready to change the money

Times change

And tables turn while Korans and Bibles burn

And we still have not learned a damn thing

I can hear angels sing

Sam Cook blended with the instruments of desperation

dancing in dirty water

Shit

You want to know the source to all the world's problems?

Black girls need fathers!

Mangled by midnight talking to toddlers dangling in the web of luciferin light

We listen to the live fiction of religion and engage in the most ignorant-ists of fights

Cause yo grandmama's grandmama's grandmama's grandmama

Used to ship Jesus juice from the bitter cup of life

Past it around like communion at the family reunion

Hand it down to yo daughters and yo sons

While the truth gets left behind like hitchhikers without thumbs

Now pump da brakes brace your face to embrace the lyrical lava

See I am simply Sundiata

The shadow of a griot who speaks for Slangston in the language of heartbeats and drums

Succumb by drama dogma and despair demonic deities doggara and death dancing in the air

I am not a priest or a preacher just a poet who speaks the truth

and that shit is rare

Now run your hand through your hair, that's the people right there

Touch the surface of the earth underneath

The thoughts caught in the roots the purpose and the prayers

Those is ghost down there

Haunting yo mind trying to find freedom

But your scalp is a plantation and the follicles that grow are the people

The slaves, the children, mothers, daughters, fathers, sons, babies, bitches and niggez

Your existence a ticket purchased in pain by the price they paid

"elegant heart beats of the sun's flame"

GOD

Her greatest gift

Locked in chains

Dyeing to live

You know I heard that Jesus was coming back

And that nigga probably is… but *write* now

SUNDIATA LIVES!!!!

ASHE' MUTHER FUCKERS!!!!

BLACK JESUS

Affirmation For Assata

Get yo hands off my Mama
you
better

When the wind whispers
those whose ears will stand
open to the opus of wisdom will listen
while most only hear their own confusion
stuck on replay
spinning history backwords
on a colonized phonograph crafted by grafted
men

The suns romantic magic
syphoned like fossil fuels
into the crude liquid emotions of lost sheep
stretched across America's
intravenously sustained nightmare
while the deaths of our realities
are survived by the memories of dead revolutionaries clawing at their
own faces in the afterlife
trying to feel something from
the soulless embrace of black apologist attempting to corn syrup shuck and fuck
their way to assimilation

transparent eyes that hide
behind the implants of Borg drones gentrified
by black Locutus
dripping Eurocentric curriculums from his orifices
like mucus and resistance is not mutual
photon torpedoes of
faithlessness fired from starship drones
at Gods Grandmother and home doesn't
exist

But if you touch my mama
I'm going kill your Jesus till his bleached skin turns black
if you harm a single hair
of
her hearts beat

I'm going shit in yo pie and piss on your cat

Freedom is Bred Internally
so the FBI can terrorize themselves
your Jim Crow encoded
holographic semantics and exercised lies
discussed as justice was not enough
to keep liberations maternal Christ in a cell
the bastard bullets lodged
in 2pacs body
have been reloaded into heavens chamber
and aimed directly
at his aunts oppressor
the waters around Cuba transmuted into golden seal
with the healing sages of a mothers tongue
dipped in Yamaha's prayers and perspiration
received from the open palms of dieing
children attempting to touch eternity breathing
with broken lungs

closed caskets carry divine
cargo
Celestial father figures
burnt out by the sun
eyelids put to bed
because if a Assata Shakur is
a terrorist
than nigga God is dead
Hands Off

Time turns back years of
incarceration there is a black liberation forever marching in the blazing embers of my hearts
furnace stoking truth
the determined derelicts of
dialectic dead diction
performing mouth 2 movement
resuscitation on the cold chest plate of
rotting negro narratives peeling back
the crusted enzymes of the minds designed incarceration

clearly you have been brainwashed
by the dust diabetes and demons
a wise man told me that the
black man never even existed
and my souls cellular conviction is compelled to

overstand the position
the philosophy of phenotypic description
placed in the confliction of submission

but my mutted senses have
awoken to open vision depicted
in the lack of balance and
truth
molding mucus from memory
coughing up cerebral plantations
complacent assimilation
swallowing slogans and digesting the noose
Lines of fire drawn in the
sands of history burning at a zillion degrees YouTube streams of dope and smoke
screen realties quoted from the mouths of revolutionary mimicry

talented tongues talk treason
in the form of opportunistic pundits peddling political slavery in exchange for
status
 to be honest your promises taste like
slave
rations
cause the masses now serve
the masses of the masters vampires drinking the blood of the blind
every man is your mirror but
you still can't find your self
whipped by biblical text we
rub coco butter on life's whelps
but if Jesus came back tomorrow
he'd text message God and ask her for help

Eliohim's children have sense
bartered off their souls divinity in exchange for swine woven garments while
Gaia chokes down the elixirs of infinity blasphemy and death
ancient priestess
holding sacred seasonings in their breasts
but the mountain top is dripping
with the rotten milk of bloody retinas and deception

you can't champion Obama and
then scream free Assata in the same breath
your tongue is tattooed with
the whispers of ancestor's blood
and broken amniotic fluid rushing the shores
of Babylon at noontime

and the oceans floor is on fire

But I believe

I believe in life
and the flow
of karmatic energy
the reincarnation of elders
as babies
and truth as blessings

I believe in my people
resurrecting themselves
with a Christ consciousness
connected intravenously
replacing cracks choreographed
government
laced legacy

I believe in grandmothers and
hands held like rituals
palms placed beneath generations

I believe in light
penetrating the ages
poems as transmissions to my daughter's
great granddaughter
the medicine of madness
exercising demons with insanity workouts
celestial memory chiseling
my akashic muscle tone like soundwaves
aimed at the minds of the wicked

because while I am a child of God
I am still a student of revolution
So you better not touch my Mama
take yo hands off my Mama

hands off

Hands Off Assata
Assasta is my Mama
Assata is our Mama
you better not touch my Mama…
nigga

The Flame

The difference between being a torch barrier and becoming the torch, is the willingness to light one's self on fire.

So on the day that my spirit decides to take leave

and leave this body behind like a weary container

no longer capable of sheltering eternity

I ask you

Please do not cremate my body, unless you burn my body of work with it

and pass on the flame to the poets who will follow me

otherwise

it would be such a waste of the fire that these words have provided me

But sometimes the future feels too heavy to hand down to its occupants

and I am just a poison predecessor of pain passing down failures to an unprepared lineage

spitting words like live worms into a baby bird's esophagus

tossing dreams like daggers back and forth with fate

leaving scorching footprints across the devils rib cage

trying to blaze a path through their own burning realties

and poetry is just embers getting cold on page

trying to remember what the warmth of our own words felt like

sacred syllables sending smoke signals to future generations

trying to craft a better tomorrow from smoldering stanzas and ash

so I am fighting while writing trying to ignite and rewrite shattered communities

for children served cup fulls of character assassination in class rooms

worldstarr hiphop and youtube injected into the airwaves of their veins like air

until their hope and aspirations explode

in a flaming spectacle of bass beat decibels and gentrification

I see ghost moon walking across the melinated faces of fatherless babies

shaken at their core trapped in emotional cages

ignorance replacing places in ribcages where hearts were left torn

but they don't want to write poems

they didn't come here to create they came here to escape

cause the places where they live are havens for hate pain and neglect

molested by memories too loud to forget

so the beats keep bumping and the streets keep humming wondering why the slums are so upset

but what am I to do walking across hot ground carrying a torch too heavy to pass down

breathing in the fumes of my own fate and the reason it's so heavy

is because it was handed to me from the hands of the greats

but so often as poets we just get open at the opus and openly masturbate

ejaculate metaphors like madness on plates and never procreate

any food for thought so young minds are dying at an alarming rate

and sometimes every word that I write just feels like a waste

knowing that my greatest inspiration won't save them

prayer beads and paintings

art is supposed to be our connection with the divine creator

not just lines confined to paper

maybe

maybe I'm not even a poet

just somebody who happens to write poetry

perhaps I'm a pagan

a magi mixed with a mason

corresponding cadences with constellations

an agent of an ancient who shape shifts through the matrix

my fire was carbon dated

Permetheous with no purpose a tragedy in the making

afraid that if I don't pass this flame to the next generation

the fire will never inspire greatness

get too hot

drop it and watch it serve as the source for my own cremation

so please don't burn my body without my body of work

don't bury my flesh, bury my text next to Fire Angelou's best verse

I want to be reincarnated in one of Rani's pages

Spread my ashes over an Armand Jackson passage

My illest lines redefined edited a thousand times in one of Daniel Wilson's rhymes

Fuck that, I'm trying to come back on a Scooby Tuck track with mo flow than CoCo and my Lyric intact

let my art in heavenly desire a legacy burning in effigy live eternally like exploding stars

in distant galaxies that no astronomy can chart

so I'll be reborn with a new anatomy understandably profound from the start

and a Lemell Powell stanza implanted beneath my chest replacing my shattered heart

poets

why we write is to create chapters of our life for the afterlife

that I'll precede us after life

hell's flames a far concern from words preserved in earnest

so light my entire epidermis like a furnace

mummify my metaphors wrapped in the notebook pages of tomorrow's greatest writers

ink injected I'm trying to be resurrected in the cadence

of Najah James, Nia Scott, Curtis and Kia Davis

let my works Gravity levitate lyrics living infinitely

reciprocated artistry kinetically arranged telekinetically

with the written imagery of Su Tin, Nicole Harrison and Shania Pinckney

spill Nommo from my quill as ill as Brion Gill

I want to write like Aerial Knight

craft epics that are metamechic and translate my poems into the language of sunlight

oragone my souls energy until I am literally electricity raising from the page

powered not by my own fires circulation but rather the inspiration we exchange

like a passed flame never to be extinguished by deaths cold

so I am ready

see this was handed to me by Baari Shabaz, Jaki Terry, Mitchel Ferguson and R.B. Jones

that's why the weight of my words are so heavy and my breath melts microphones

"making the fire that's inside me a fire that's beside me my passion to write a fuel"

light myself on fire like Richard Pryor

and let my inspiration serve as the greatest cremation ever

experienced on stage

as you witness me pass on

the flame

A Poor Man's Dream

"ray light morning fire lynch, yester pain in dreams comes again"

opening like eyelids resistant to the existence of realities persistent gleam
and struggle seems to require an immunity to truth
just to swallow the late night placebos of poetry and faith
and survival often tastes like surrender setting on the tongue tips of forgotten battlefields
where creativity rises like fresh flowers in bloom
from the womb beneath lifeless cadavers

Babylon's babies babbling beneath the whisper of a crumbling family structure
this city is an angry bitch who sits on dreams like prayers carved into porcelain
shitting out nightmares, cause poverty stinks
reeks of rotten children and steaming piles of decomposing regrets
decaying carcasses cradled too violently in the sobering embrace of madness
like the murdered bodies of dead possibilities feeding the trees like demented photosynthesis
like snapped photos of sins with a focused synthesis on death

dead flesh feeding the fertile soil of futures like fertilizer
for a city that endlessly imitates the imagery of cemeteries skyscrapers like tombstones
blades to veins bleeding out poetry
prophets praying while we write hoping that we might profit from her pain and save souls
eulogies encrypted in the concretes bones
cracks filled with crack where childhoods grow to spite
the odds of heroin laced legacies
squeezed in between the seams of devilish diversity
I have
personally witnessed
some of the best people
living in the worst conditions

like babies teething for nourishment seething squeezing onto severed umbilical cords with broken teeth
biting off the ear lobes of Edgar Allen Poe's pedantic pedophilic memory
spitting revisionist history on a filthy fructose laced dinner plate

we are decayed sacs of water and notebook paper
walking through tunnels without light
dead poets trying to write ourselves back to life

and death often feels like muted dreams
but maybe our load ugly truth
is just the recipe for a diet of quit beautiful lies
disguised as opportunity
our frustration and hatred blooming beside orchards of budding hope

the wire in her chest
the birds feeding off her flesh
exploding from beneath the wrinkles in old black ladies faces

we live like dying orphans
tongues tattooed to our mother's breast
swallowing poison milk until we choke on the neglect

from people who scowl like confused owls at each other's pigment
as if our differences aren't trapped under the same chain yoked into submission
so blessed in our shittiest conditions
fertilizing faith from a forgotten future on fire

cause the truth is simply urine disguised as orange juice
inside of a cracked shot glass
art dripping, poetry dripping, the dead bodies of poets and musicians dripping
from a hell soaked salvation that somehow serves
as the source of our greatest inspiration
because sometimes life is just the nightmare from which
we haven't yet awakened
A poor man's dream, forsaken

I watched a tired teary eyed mother gazing
At a skyline made of one act stage-plays and instruments
Meant to double in double time as the drug of life
Dripping from the heaven laced veins of an angel
disguised as a solar system
With permed hair, gentrification spreading like cancer across her epidermis
The ice queen of death and invisible purpose

But we call her
Baltimore

True Blood

Sleep
Water rising beyond the margin
Spirit in the woods
Sunrays
Dawn morning street
Quiet house
Naked praise song
Baptist hymn
Liquor store racists in da south
Cemetery sex snake bit
Vines grow around the machine
Hate grows older in a flash
Children eat hearts with bloody lips
American flag in the night cupped tittes naked mixed girl
Possum road kill. Men speak for God.
Fuck your women by the pool table
Black man praising 360 sanctified spin
Crucified vampires your prayers go unanswered
devil stripper
Amphibious reptiles feed the trap for Venus
Snap
Christ burning the wolf comes back from the dead
With maggots as flesh fighting orgies and religion
Devil lays hand on goddess
Alien out the chrysalis anointed by false prophets
Holy ghost chant and leap booty shake back seat
Inhale the smoke through the succubus's lips
Witches baptized in bad things running from the saints
Sex the morning love the night
The madman as prophet trying to find himself by jumping outside of self
Shed seven skins and soul searched through star walks
The mountain begs the trees for drugs
A fix to find God and ask for the questions
Swallowed the answers and spit out the cosmos
Thoughts are deception wrapped in this water and dust outfit
I go in by going out, ascend to the underground to war with my dragon
Shapes of form matter is illusion energy is truth atoms in my flesh
Who thus dance on the ocean floor with death and fuck life once a moon
The sun is coming back
The man who was son God birthed planet spinning into crucified implosion
Sucked into the mouth of uncountable universes

you can't even calculate the sands
of Time
Invisible hands clock digital creator deities
on their knees smashing the ants
Eye and the shaman swallowed the lord's flesh at the sermon on mount
Intergalactic falacio drinking the nectar of infinity constellations circling through
lifetimes
Blood bend a billion heartbeats onto blank pages
Hemorrhaging light
I have met God, and they are Us
Eternal vibrational beings
Blended into stars dust
Your face goes here

When a city burns and children scream in flames
Riots turn into the language heard by otherwise closed ears
Harriet Tubman sings freedom songs to the soul of
Frederick Douglas
Watching waves of solidarity march past the harbor at dawn
We protested with poem filled lungs
Now stanzas ignite silence into results
And white guilt is my spirit animal
We bled for this
We bled for this
We bled for this
And history is a freedom song that makes me murder the radio
Murder your voice box with lies as playlist
Murder your mouth for the narrative you rewrote as blasphemous note
To a song we never sung with liberated tongues
So now every rhythm is a prophecy
And every word your death
Uprising until our lives are given respect
Oh you thought you knew blood.

Like you knew
God.

N.I.G.G.A.

"powerful people cannot afford to educate the people that they oppress
because once you are truly educated
you will not ask for power.
You will take it." –John Henrik Clarke

Slave hymn in your stomach
Broken bible verse in your pocket
The watch that watches time while in motion like the redline
Riding towards your heartbeat
The stolen over priced soul that you can't buy back played back on repeat

The soul beneath our feet screams secrets
Enslaved voices screeching orisha's singing the song of death
There are silent auctions held inside your mothers chest
For the tectonic fetal tissue that will be your offspring's
Future planting earthquakes in our children's path
before they can take their first steps

barcodes branded on new born babies birth certificates
there is a price set on your life's worth
selling yourself back to your self
before you can download your self worth

there is an app that interacts with your melanin
but you gotta die first

there is dirt in my dialogue
and a "callous on my soul"

scratching at the infection like a mad turntabalist
a bloody crucifix carved into my fingerprints
demonic dogma bleeding from our lips
cause lord knows when the cock crows
they will take hold and cyphen the God out of your dick

Steve Biko's spirit sits dormant inside the consciousness of black light
Waiting to awake Soweto at night so "I write what I like"

Yea nigga
Hey nigga
Nigga what
My nigga

I am so fucking tired of treating the truth like an apology
Battling desolation with dead platforms and outdated philosophy's

Fuck you, and fuck them too!

There is no time for holding hands and marching in reverse
At a time when fists should be gripped and raised in righteous rebellion
My cosmic footprint outdates your by billions
Everything you've ever thought of we already did first
Had celestial swag before you ever called this place earth
Fuck you Miley Cyrus I hope your ass explodes the next time you try to twerk

We create both commerce and culture but something is fucking wrong
If we are God than how come we still follow slave protocols
Black rappers claim new slave
While white mc's proclaim to be rap gods

I am Jesus at a peaceful protest fully strapped
I am John Brown posting pics on instagram of freed slaves being sold back
I am Harriet Tubman in the club making it clap
I am Imhotep on crack
I am your worst fucking nightmare
cause I don't know who eye am
But I know how to I.M.

A biracial binary baby with an I phone plugged into his navel
Keeping Africa fully charged
Only to get charged double
For the price of my life back
And catch a charge from those in charge
Charged with no rights
So your damm right its within my rights to write back

Nigga…
Frederick Douglass aint need twitter
(and he's being recognized more and more now days)

We be revolutionary as shit with a like and a click on Facebook
But rarely face books
Read the writing on the walls tagged by Babylon
You've been marked for extinction
Call it destiny or death
Prophesy or lack of access
Regardless our lives are on the line
But everyday you stay on line everywhere you @
So how the fuck you lack access

searched the engine and highlighted the text
I saw Dubois and Garvey i-pads plugged into Baldwin's pigment
Downloading Africa's heartbeat

Langston Hughes laughs at the legacy laid by
Creative cultural capitalists in his name
Trying to corner your organs and gentrify your intestines
Cause the body of god is hardly gOD'S BODY when the God body are just as
Corrupt as the devils be
So do the knowledge b
Or rather Deuteronomy

Universal Laws divine energy and ancient astrology
5th dimension gifted
I channel the jewels in opened wounds
And commune with Countee Cullen's spirit
When I'm on the number 3

But it seems new slaves are just old slaves with new chains
And from louie to coogee, fendi and prada
We still pick cotton just the same

2 Chainz goes platinum
while Laruen Hill went to prison
and the dumb deaf and blind don't even have ears to hear
the inbondaged conditions
of their own indignant "Consumerism"
HipHop got butt raped by the platinum incrusted dick of industry snakes
but make to mistake
the truth can't be faked

Nigga…
don't believe me just watch
Stars all on my clock
Fuck yo trinity I spit divinity
Theology in my watch
Nigga Nigga Nigga Nigga Nigga

We always after the white water cause the white water equates to the good water
The good music
the good hair
the good skin
The good schools that I'm trying to put my 2 kids in

You could be Travon Martin Delany King
And still not be accustomed to the hood you in
They put Christ in a hood and let the media crucify the spin
But when the zealots was finished yelling
We remain equally
Unaware of the blood spilling in the linen and the linage of the hood you in
So if you "Brown" six shots I'll put you down for the count
Cause your very skin is seen as a threat to the world you in

We create culture they copy the contents
And sale it back
Extract the black and sale it back
As consumers we carry the weight of what we create on our back
They sale it back

Versace Versace Versace Versace Versace
As consumers we carry the weight of our fate on our back
They sale it back
Africa Africa Africa Africa Africa

I guess the Griot is back with a vengeance
I don't want to be included and I'm not trying to be intrusive
White guilt had sex with white privilege and produced assimilated niggez

Pork on your fork
Swine killing niggez
Police out in force
Swine killing niggez

Niggez niggez where all my niggez
Niggez be getting paper
Niggez be on the move
Niggez be on YouTube niggez stay on the news
Live in front of the camera getting shot with they crew
Niggez be in Paris
Niggez be in Africa too

While the children of Patrice Lumumba remain locked in chains
And the Congo gets raped for all the diamonds, gold and coltan
Niggez will never change aint shit that you can do
A million martyrs slain
Black Jesus got shot to death by a tech loaded with karma cashed checks
The resurrection never came

You've been deceived if you believe anybody gives a fuck if you breathe
Dr Sebi cured cancer,aids and diabetes
Nobody recorded reported or handed out any vaccines
Nigga Please…

Compliance with colonialism only leads to regression
Desegregation deconstructed our best weapons
But we still haven't learned the lesson
We don't need progression in exchange for acceptance

But in our minds white still equals wealth
When the true wealth is in your cells
But we still ask for access
To what is already apart of our selves
When really what we need is to access our self

You can't be in the struggle and not struggle

I found my purpose on purpose
Turned verses into churches
Meditate mold metaphors into meaning
Beat-boxed with out breathing

Spoke with the tongue of a heathen
Cadence crafted from bible pages and the dialect of demons
Until words became flesh

That's when niggez started eating
Religion became cannibalism
Take the flesh and the blood nigga eat it

Cause babies are birthed by God but niggez are of men
Turned his umbilical cord into a noose and let loose what was within
The Nigga
But God is within my niggez

If David Walker walked right in
In this very instance
He wouldn't appeal he'd kill
In the name of the niggez

So every word I'm writing is in the name of every slain nigga
See God is pissed as shit and she wants back her stolen niggez

"there is a railroad of bones at the bottom of the ocean"

there is a chamber of souls in the guns our sons are holding
there is a loud graveyard planted beneath every American
city
there are a billion black bodies coming back to the living

you thought the zombie apocalypse was some shit
just wait until you get a hold of my niggez

see this is the dispensation of truth in the nu age
and there are so many slain ancestors coming back for revenge
that it I'll make reparations look like minimum wage

but they control the water the air and the planes
the radioactive rays that rearrange your thought waves
so a 12 gage held to every hybrids brain
is the only way we ever going see any true change

we don't need you if you trying to be them
we don't need you if you trying to be in their skin
more than the skin you in

the time tic is over
rearrange your circuitry
with keylontic synergy
stretch memory with Kemetic yoga
the hermetic soul controller of meta and matter
at the center of the galaxy inside the hue-man heart beat
just trying with all our might to relight a dead sun (son)

no justice to peace

but i will scream justice in this piece
if it is just us in this piece
but don't expect no just us
once we take to the streets

black lives don't matter
black lives are matter

you know
like black
like space
like stars and shit
melanin, matter
nigga

"Naturally Intellectual Ghetto Galactic Alchemists"

N.I.G.G.A.

but sometimes I wonder if it all really matters
when I hear the devils laughter
and if dreams are just nightmares that haven't shattered

a wise man once told me
that the Blackman is God
if God looked into a mirror
and the mirror shattered

Kuumba

Just because it could be worse
doesn't mean
that it shouldn't
be better

Kuumba

"Al-Qalam Nun

                                                  By the pen and what we write

                                            By the pen and what the angels write

By the pen

I swear I am not a mad man"

Al-Qalam

Kuumba

                                            "By the pen and what the angels write"

And with this piece I channel just a small piece
Of the creator
So that with every line that I write
I design my own life
You create reality

God's wisdom written within my compositions
In which to write life into existence
For God is all
And within us we each possess just a small spark Through our art

One part

A single smidgen that mimics the infinite

and I as imperfect as perfect
searching for purpose in these verses
in between lines where life takes precedence
and words become worthless

And the universe can be felt
On the tip of self help

Cause there are some things
that need to be changed
about myself

That are preventing me
from producing positive movements
in the direction of my own wealth

Stomach filled with starving stanzas
Scraping the insides of divine hunger pains

And sometimes I just want to leave this place

Every moment/*mourning* facing the mirror
staring into my father's face

And sometimes poetry processes such a sour taste
but out of the necessity for clarity we create

Pens penetrate apathy
rendering injuries into ravenous rationalities
Giving children back their right to write
and incite creativity

In the sight of incorrect correction
I color outside the lines
To realign your minds indirect perception

Placed beneath still waters
we can see God's reflection

"so read in the name of the lord

who creates us from a clot

Who by the pen taught men what we knew not"

And the waters run deep
So into the distance of the infinite I reach
To seek the light
Crying at night with struggle on repeat
I tried to write my life into the beat

But every day is another day to keep trying

To be a better me

And when it happens it hurts
Blurred tears and slurred thoughts stir
As the earth continues to turn
And I wish that I could capture the whole world
Just so I could share it with her

So no longer will I pray
but thank
the most high
for what has already been done

Past present and future all one

Because

                                                     "only lower density lifeforms get lost in time"

We are all artists
with the ability to create ourselves
in each line

No need for

faith

fate
destiny
or dogmatic religious recipes

I am God and so are we

Infinitely divine
Able to shine
inside
the most high's light

Because through the creator's gifts when given
We have the ability to create and make
Ourselves
Into whatever we want to be
Why do you think it's called creativity?

Therefore what I write is my life
Ignite it and recite it into position
I write my entire world into existence
Spit it and then live it

"Al-Qalam

Kuumba

Nun

                                                                                     By the pen and what we write

By the ink stand and the pen

And that which thy write

By the grace of thy lord

Tho art not a mad man

I swear by the pen

                                                                                      And what the angels write"

Alkaluum

Kuumba

"By the pen and what the angels write"

Alkaluum Kuumba

Create yourself

Create

Yourself

Alkebulan

I remember when she used to pull heaven from the sky like fresh baked bread upon request

laid my life in her footsteps
fingerprints gently placed over my face
gliding across times recline with a divine caress
taken to the tip of my earlobes consoled interest
and lovingly pressed

so that I might hear the harmonic mnemonics
in her heart's stress

phonetic fiber optics
locked inside her 3rd eye socket
so that on sight every page that I write remains blessed
even when in the presence of death and unrest
she speaks life
for she is life traced back to its very onset

genetically brilliant
with the physical architecture
of ancient buildings
hips thicker
than the wisdom in scriptures
with the spiritual resilience
of apocalyptic bomb threats

raped by imperialism's jizim
to the point of non-recognition
and she bares the pain
like slave remnants

but what is a mother to do
when her children have practiced
how to master the art of neglect
beyond disrespect
globally disconnected
unable to see her
inside of our own reflection

and the same goes for many of those
who still take abound in her home
paralyzed by time
rebellious without cause
you cannot whitewash the soul of the most high

she is the most beautiful woman of all time
and I love her dearly
so much that it scares me
where my ears meet where her heart beats
I hear me
I see us
In between hatred and trust
naked with no lust
the Nommo in her womb flows
up throats
through microphones
like lost info
about

US

This verse persists until only my dreams exist
and our lips unify liquefied bliss choreographed into a first kiss
Healing the village with nation building between hips
our children's children's legacy in a melody
you cannot sale your cellular memory
celestial ancestral ecstasy
recipes

remember this

the griots grip extended spitting the restored stories of
history's true image replenished
until
heaven's highest helix
is extended
her birth canal connected to the Nile like
Kush
Nubia
and Kemet

my purpose nourished through the invisible umbilical mic cable
wrapped around our navels
inserted into her cervix that's why my verses are so vivid
even the ones from my past life
so in reality everything that I write has already been written
depicted in Sybil visions

words scripted on the broken wings
of dieing ghetto birds
lying in dirty gutters
trying to fly back to our mothers

and my entire epidermis aches for her embrace
I see her features burning on the surface
of every black woman's face

so the truth remains hidden

history rewritten by the temples thieves
more than Eve
but rather the celestial rib
splitting atoms
in Adam's place
caged in by faith

and it seems so useless
the way she fights life with no armor for usage
yet still never loses
and the whole world abuses
the rhythms within her children's
sacred music

his-story tries to hide us
perception of deception provided
like the conflict residing behind diamonds

so we sale are $ouls jewels to fools
while civil wars divide us
as cells dividing like ooze inside primordial pools

and like love

we are the lost ones

gone

scattered

unable to translate the language
of the drum patterns
in our own songs
and you may know her
by her slave name of Africa
but I remember when
Eye remember when

We called her Alkebulan

Oshun's Revenge

sometimes i see spirits
breakdancing on the closed eyelids
of sleeping infants...

waiting

anticipating
thee awakening

all the animals have evacuated
from out of your imagination

conjuring chaotic catacombs created to correspond callously configuring containment
concocted from Caucasian cocks cocked fired and reloaded in succession in the direction of
celestial ancestors causing my mothers, mothers, mothers, mothers, mothers
clitoris to travel forward through a time portal
and pimp smack some sanctified sense
into yo bitch ass

a storm is brewing!

beaconing like ravenous multiple metaphysical orgasms splashing crashing flashing like
lightning igniting re-writing the recitings of your bastard ass nation inside the vesica pisces of
divine creation re-making shaping energy mana matter mangled metaphors morphed into
vaginal vengeance
i em sea like red seas given instant division spitting wide open oceans overflowing from the
womb
of Oshun's menstrual liquids

point blank period. end of sentence.

witness a re-birth at its bloody beginning
see there will never be peace in our lifetimes unless first negotiated in accordance with the
terms of unrecorded war crimes reported from front lines while M.L.K. lays in his grave
holding a loaded 12 gage awaiting the day when he'll be

free to blast
free to blast
thank God almighty
i'm a blast yo white ass!

my notebook has exploded

and only one page remains

declaring that your dicks and your guns
shall be castrated in the name
of the mother the daughter
and the son/sun
that they raised!

there will be no more black martyrs
baptized in unholy illumanati waters
word to the "ghetto alphabets" author
because "God is not an American"
and neither were your forefathers!

and i am your worst nightmares, worst nightmare

awake!

and aware, well prepared

take pathetic poets focused on the fact that they getting noticed expose em remold fold and roll em leave em in a time loop like samples for beats loaded into mpcs for mcs
and leave em there…

on repeat

still spewing the same useless pseudo conscience nonsense that "jewish" white people with pensions been exploiting for years and if you just applauded you was probably exactly who i was talking about up in here

shhhhhhhhhhhhhhhhhhhhhhhhhhhhhhhhhhhhhhhhhhhhhhhhhhhhhhhhhhhhhhhhhhhhhhh
sawhooooooooooooooooooooooooooooooo saaaaaaaaaaaaaaaaa sewhhhhhhhhhhhhh
shhhhhhhhhhhhhhhhhhhhhhhhhhhhhhhhhhhhhhhhhhhhhh su shhhhhhhhhhhhhhhhhhhhhhhhhh
SHIT!

tsunami temper tantrums washing away
the industries inventions, rapist religions and politicians conditioned with shallow and pedantic answers following justice at the feet of just-us trying to feed-us from the fetus of the drum festivals flyest dancers

so now as the age shifts again your civilization is drowning in Darwin's Christian sin see this is just a MESSAGE that i recorded with the goddess' pen
she nourished you with knowledge loved you with wisdom massaged light into your triple darkness and gave you life yet you perceived kindness as weakness bloodied her beauty with bondage and now her intimacy has become vengeance

witness the scorned wrath of a woman writing hieroglyphic graffiti on the walls of her womb
woven into words that no sound can transmit
with clinched fists baptizing the planet's surface

verses written in tears and sealed in the sky with a kiss

while the water calls for the moon to crash into a cliff and shooting stars drift through the abyss
as the sun drips levite lava from drama filled pen tips white yoga instructors checking they horoscopes
trying to find out if they sign switched
like oh shit (well i was a Pieces but now i'm a Sagittarius, what the fuck is this bullshit)

cause the cosmos is yo babies mama
and karma is a bitch

and you ain't never

heard a love poem
like this!

Sagefo's Words

"Correspondence with ourselves

and our Black family

We read magic

now we need the spells, to rise up

return, destroy and create. What will be

the sacred words?"- Amiri Baraka

Yo yo yo yo yo yo yo yo yo

I don't know about ya'll but I'm fitting on getting

out of here

Not here but here, I'm where?

I am not here, I am no one or no where

Except Aware

That this earthly collection of blood flesh and bones is nothing but clothes

Epidermis material inclosing the flame centered furnish of the spiritual

Melanated metaphysical ether garments enslaved dirt and water walking

Temporary coffins locked in to def (death) tones unable to hold this soul because energy remains eternal

Lyrical vibration turning verbels at the speed of life

Recite a divine sacred cadence of ancient incantations with linear lines

Capable of getting you higher than dime bags of herbals

I'm fly wit da flow

No you don't understand I can fly with my flow

Reach out and touch the sky when I flow

It's the ghetto griot speech lethal

stanzas stacked with enough heat to leave

33rd degree burns on the ass checks of the devil

from lashes of fantastic intergalactic wordplay

they say Satan's salad tossers want to cut off half my tongue

to keep my mouth from running away like Kunta Kinte

but you shall not de-feat (feet) these rebels

Regenerated resonance reactivates reawakened revolutionary radio frequencies

from metaphors manufactured with medu-mecha telepathy

Liberation lyricism ripping through stereo systems in direct contention sound check chin checking consecutive ignorance from laminated knowledge that's limited head nodding yo noggin

slaves to the rhythm following the calling of college only to major in self separation

slaves studying synthetic fissanary caucasian civilizations in preparation for assimilated living

tap dancing on our ancestors shoulders while
rich white folks applaud the latest rhythmic renditions

nigga listen

this is spoken nuclear fusion using my hearts
drum patterns
tracing constellations translating the universes
sacred music divine blueprints

verses born in the form of celestial vocal vestibules

this be that uncut that God constructs to touch thee untouched

unseen poetic rhyme schemes spitten with the vivid image of an inner paintbrush

and evolution is imperative so my fingerprints were printed with the sacred meanings hidden in the
scarred harmonies of slave narratives you can feel the field songs in my larynx

so no amount of money can meaningfully merit this experience

explosive quoted spoken soul visions transmitted from the star system of Sirius

Dogon drum beats speak to me in my sleep
dreams hunted by cellar memory

my spirit energy inherits me with the ability to channel God, Great Grandma and Infinity

moving around Saturn with poetic patterns of Kemetic symbolism

dipped in cryptic lyricism initiated in ancient mystery

Slangston be the spoken word Selassie spitting forbidden philosophy

And believe me this flesh is not my final destination

Cerbel Dj spinning Mahalia on a vinyl compilation

Freedom reborn in the form of a crack addicted b-boy on the tip of my tongue braking

and I can taste it driving me creatively crazy cotton caught in my cadence

cause I swear every rap song I hear sounds like
the screams of Sarah's baby

New Orleans and Haiti attached to her back

Cause even in this millennium whips still crack

It's like the song of Sagefo keeps calling us back

and I know if I reach deep enough into myself I can make contact

so I'm going in

all the way to in

to where middle passage passengers play out the drum patterns to planet rock in polyrhythmic syncopation

blessings and messages reflected through sound waves deflected through ocean graves

directed at shot up blocks

inner city plantations where children play the role of cast out hated and tainted on corners

cast in the mold of concrete cages where bullets serenade rib cages

sirens parading like invading aliens

blue lights beckoning bastardized babies bathing in blinged out blankets of bereavement

baptized in the broken waters of crack coded wombs on the bodies of Babylonian bitches beat boxing hieroglyphic tunes as times divine baseline echoes through Christ's empty tomb

while Osiris sues for royalties from religion's remixed African track

because God has returned and she wants her fucking shit back

and I already told you that I do not live here

so I had to go in, no not in but I mean I really went in

and I'm not coming back!

Beyond transatlantic continental shifting this isn't even my planet
Metaphysics mingled with madness God damn it I can't stand it
Sagefo's words stranded
in between my stanzas

somebody said Slangston seems to have gone insane

and it feels like Isis is writing the diagnosis on my page in a rage

while little miniature Harriet Tubman's are walking into viginas like caves

performing abortions on black babies just to prevent the birth of more slaves

because you still refuse to embrace your own greatness

beyond spoken word this is Egyptian symbolism translated into Hebrew hieroglyphics

spitting light transmissions in the cadence of constellations breaking into ancient foundations reawakening our D.N.A.'s sacred vibration

incantations causing pages to resonate with the frequency of the most high

ripping in the rhythm of remembrance my molecules spinning faster than warp engines

indigo flow poems composed in the words of Sagefo so fuck rhyme schemes we be star-seeds

spitting light-beams in the direction of the competition

shit don't even need a mother-ship

I'm walking to the next dimension

word to Saul Williams "warrior women's wombs

still waiting for the greatest Americans to be incarnated"

and preparation is my mission

stepped on stage and ascended

I'm Gone!!!!!!!!!

Now who's coming with me?????????

Sundiata Strikes Back

Dismantled villages do not raise good children

The elders are dieing and no one ever stopped to listen to their wisdom

Many/mini men have become thee equvilent of gargantuan
infants, bullshit

Forget this, malnutrition educational systems resembling bull-whips

Entire diaspora exasperated in continental sized
slave ships as the age shifts

Lion prints tattooed across my wrists yo interest is counterfeit monetary metaphoric moorish content crushing caucasian terrorist camera lenses before their inhibitions get the open instant to flick

Pose for souls told to expose their own inclosed intentions vicious conventions clothed in brainwashed loads of ignorance

Enter the center linger language little singer strangers gentrified chicken fried south beach diet danger heat bangers socks shot through hangers wicked wizard wordplay behaviours synchronize tantalized tentative talents talons gripping the challenge around in i'm bound with ice chains whips enemies surrounded shots rounded unfounded until the smallest child found it prayed 4 pennies 4 thoughts tossed into youth fountains truth unbounded i'm down with Douglass Gravy Marley Drew Ali Mohammad Mosses P. Newton Turner shooting reloaded freedom producing Balal style modern Mali hardly obviously odyssey records the last epic accepted assassinated the hated in seconds but nobody took notes on the last lesson

I swear

i saw Africa

in my dreams

baptized in bleaching cream code orange complexion rocking a free guchi t shirt bobbing her head 2 deception

with giant blood diamonds as headphones volume controlled by stereo-types shuffling confusion

use my words to mute the music

cause the succession of oppressions generational connections run deep spoiled monastery missionaries resurrecting crucifixes on blood stained soil like morning erections

so we recite nightmare scenes into mics in an attempt to shake up the dice i tried to wake up to my life yet had never gone to sleep... out of money still hungry here's some words you should eat

Freedom is like death when slavery becomes the sweetest option left

futuristic scriptures composed from ancient text so i guess i'm Sundiata coming back to the ghetto with a loaded teck...

Sogolon Y chromosomes preserved in my poems with precision

9 dimensions of pimping metaphysics inventions solicit silenced criminal ceremonial wishes the testimonial constituents sense this medium modium was invented to give em telepathic training in an instant solution polluted retribution revolution consumers using stupid useless blueprints with Lucifer dining on swine disguised as a divine 2 peace with extra grease and 3 biscuits... trinity mystery since sicily convinces me of empathy for infantry who pitted instantly listening to bastard catholic christenings by jews at the armada taking shahada baptized in the aids infested blood of a hillbilly hippie calling himself Christ telling perverted clergy pulpit pedipiles to come to the light, yeah right... im' like

I'm like a lion one of the greatest...
you're like Linus dragging his blanket
stagnant and uncreative
clothed in your ego and insecurities
I came on stage naked like Grandma David
but let's stick to the basics

if I throw a pen at you while your on the mic

it ain't cause you nice

it's cause I was aiming

for your windpipe

While wooden ankhs massage the necks of pseudo conscience poetic prostitutes
lyrically lip smacking
so my pen is pimp smacking
some spoken word farce-ists
just yapping
yall sound worse than the rappers

niggez been poets for like one year
and they trying to grandstand
mad cause they writing not strong enough
to win em a slam
so you try to switch the perspective on the profession

backwards

I'll send him back peace treaty terms
in his own words
but until you listen to this verse in reverse
and translate every word
while it's facing you

back-words

you'll just be the last first
to still not understand

Definition of a poet
I'm Gill Scott talking to 2-Pac
transmute my mic into a glock
firing shots until the top pops off of the T.E.O.P. technically efficient omnipresent potency
provoked by poetic powers

MMMMMMMM mamamamama Mathematics is average

but savage mcs mics might still grab it and hand em an old fashioned romancing ass handing for saying that what was written was heavenly I readily rise reenergized ripping rhymes rendered ridiculous renaissance rhythms resonate rings and rocks bells original LL remix renditions

you aint spitting you just spitting
saliva with no convictions
like team Denver bnv final stage remixes

Yall aint shit while I'm reppin with a pen as a weapon
my poems encoded in BIG SEVENS
making the crowd say OOH
like the late great from Brown F.I.S.H.
child of the most high like Jah
so don't confuse this
it's Mr Hughes and not Slick
you think you the shit dog... I electrify em like mic Vic... just sick with the wordplay

I mean it's all for "the love of poetry"
until egos come into play
and finances come your way
and the dj can't get his pay

so erotic poems got the audience wide open
dome swollen rollin in they own cum stains

poets love to shoot of at the lip
but won't swallow what they spit

so go a Head
get pissed
act intense
try to rip

"THIS IS MADNESS"

you ain't a Last Poet
you a lost poet
style so crazy maybe
I should be laying on a couch
but when standing in front of this mic
the stage is mine
shit you disagree with a line
you could respond in kind
but if you respond in rhyme
I'm a rip yo tongue out

you could die in your sleep
with an Obama speech on repeat

and would still fail to reach the level of awareness possessed when I unleash straight beast
lurking through jungles of concrete
leaving the pavement cracked
had Lion King swag way before Simba
so don't get Mali whopped on the track
somebody better tell em that Sundiata is back

Fiiiiiiiiiiiiiire the sacred arrow that I got from my griot
at worthless merchants with verses whose only purpose is submerging they purses in more de niro, yo I'm James Earl Jones live lion on my shoulder stepping out of the limo...
we ghetto super heros with metaphors smacking the surface like meteors man got my poetic powers from outer space like Meteor Man... with poems that are golden so don't get scolded by these lords... words break dance like emcees on water spitting brolic knowledge... Baltimore babies baptized in blood streets sanctified from the slaughter

Mmmmmmmmmmmmmmmmmmm madd magical maniacal manic anti-mantan made pages by boom bap sages made ageless passed god flesh in the flask liquefied intensified venereal venomous vehement vigorous vicious victimless verses verbose verbal vitamins from death valley walls of jericho surrounded by jehovah witnesses $aleing sweet potato pies filled with sumerian scriptures

The skies falling... and I got my God up... babylon is falling... and I don't give a fuck

So what... words live!

With Slang from my heart my language became my art
just to tear the stage apart

Paint potent poetic pictures from pain at its pen-nacle

cause fate and destiny was the recipe fed to me through thee umbilical

maybe that's why after birth I was so miserable

took years for me to even speak a single syllable

nobodies poetry compares to me I am truly an individual

a part of four who all pour from the core of thee original

This is street poetry
not because it's poetry merely primarily
for or from the streets
but because evidently
I want every single word that I speak
to eventually become concrete

One mic one life one love

everything I could budge

carved into the stars

and the gods above

In it to win it with regenerative vengeance a menace intended to give it without commission i'm finished deepest thoughts tended to tentatively turn tantrums into tornados time traveled through mic cables with verses as sacred as the universe's navel... word to plato posting shadows on the wall move across galactic skies with celestial graffiti from Sirius B to DC believe me we are more than we seem with the power to dream rhyme schemes etched into the breeze by the supreme so just breathe

And let your light shine make the darkness devine

And it ain't where you from it's where you be

fuck abstract my train of thought is alien

verses written controversial-y metaphysical lyrical spiritual poetic pleiadian I don't rep DMV I represent universally I don't spit to the beat the beat follows me chaotic yet creative cadence coded in concrete

But all of this is "just words" and speech
word to Lab
cause "without evolution revolution is obsolete"

On my raphael da la ghetto shit with Tennyson tendencys blasting cannons left and right what I write is deep

so

"listen, to the street beat

hear the sound pound

plug yo ears

mask yo fears

somethin weird's going down

so listen to the street beat

listen to the barks shark

listen

or I kill ya"

Ghetto Griot

I envy people who work at Walmart

Instead of starve for their art

auction blocking hopping for an optioned price on mics

And instead get to punch out at a normal time 5 or 9 in spite of the grind then go back to their normal life

 it I'd probably be easier if I just worked at Save-A-Lot
Or Rite Aid
at least they know exactly when their going get paid

Hand me back my chains
freedom is not worth it
poetry looks perfect on paper
But some days I can bearly afford toilet paper
what the hell

It would make so much more sense if I just worked in retail cause art is all sacrifices and the best writing don't even $ale

give me some cabin rations and a field itinerary seriously can I please just be a $lave? This social structure of convoluted confusion and human pollution is not conducive to independent thought and free action trapped in

talent and vision with lack of savvy business extensions is obviously thee equivalent of a disease entertainment does not equal elevation nigga please

HipHop in the mainstream rocks rhyme schemes to Willie Lynch themes and it seems that the rap industry is adjacent to the arrangement of plantation scenes

I mean, why you think so many mcs be hanging around high on trees

You think I be writing bars and hooks how the fuck you figga

More like composing symposiums and books I'm an intellectual nigga

And honestly what the fuck is poetry
a bunch of shallow and pedantic
ass bastards with massive theatric stage antics yapping about their hardships

talking over nonsense topics of which they have no actual knowledge

Bloviated vocal masturbation lyrically
I think I hate spoken word poetry
cause everybody sounds like this and does that, well not me
theoretically my brand is much closer to spoken imagery
Intergalactic text messaging I channel the ALL through mics
Universal nights and weekends freedom speaking through the deepest secretions of your subconscious content stream

You might write a little bit recite on mics with wit from here to the Hollywood strip

Exposed by TV shows and YouTube hits repeatly but in all honesty

Word to E you punk "P.O.P. poets" don't even exist to me sense we obviously do not

Sit on the same freaking frequency

Verbal ammo dismantling towers of Babel

And if you ask me the god Taalam Acey remains king of the spoken word scene

Because I'm too broke to travel

And music is vibrationaly so consistently therapeutic

See recently a sista asked me
"Slangston Hughes how do you do it?"

and I responded with all due humility

I don't

ghost ghostwrite for me

but monetarily those who view the world through a
"Groit's Eye"

never seem to get their full worth paid forward on time

what a dysfunctional oddisee cause unfortunately all the enlightenment

just feels like nonsense to me

how I'm going free the people when I can't even liberate myself from fucking poverty

I swear I'm about to start staring crackers dead in they face with no mask

Truth on full blast!!!!

wait

Are you trying to fuck me in my ass?

are you trying to fuck me in my ass?

Stop the poem!!!

I mean its one thing to try and fuck me over

But you not just going bend me over and fuck me in my ass

Nigga I aint Quincy Jones you cant fuck me in my ass

Useless cracker ass crackers constantly trying to fuck the black man

In his ass

for hope of a melanin transfusion

lower chakra music confusion

On blast, butt naked baby oil painted Baphomet on your latest sex fest set

With a pork flavored dildo ramming rapping sambos in they ass

Yo seriously way beyond conspiracy are you spiritually trying to fuck me in my ass

Don't get behind me Satan!!!!

You can't fuck me in my ass... Biiiiiiiiitch

I walk a righteous path!!!!!!

Now all of a sudden every pseudo conscious negro

want to stick they filthy heads down in the rabbit hole

talking about kinetic karate, illuminati

and how Kanye, Jay and Bey must of sold they souls

frozen in a westernized yoga pose

if you really knew the truth and how deep it goes

your muther fucking head would explode

this is far from spoken word or spitting verses I'm living in my purpose

what you witness is more than just a poet poking around on the surface

I am a philosophers stone in the form of a person

transmute myself into light and fight the good fight against my own life but it feels like they'll never know

and sometimes I just get so depressed with the reality

that I have to wake up everyday and be me unapologetically

It's funny how we call each other family and fam
but when the shit really hits the fan
you'll be surprised how few people actually act like fam

so hell yea I'm fucking envious of ya'll niggez
pitching in masters kitchen for pork privileges
health care plans and Uncle Sam benefits

cause I already know, that if I was murdered for what I wrote?

I wouldn't be a martyr, no movement started on behalf of my slaughter

Just eventually fade into memory while the enemy continues to grow

And it would be so beautiful to just live inside of a cubical and die slow

Because sometimes, sometimes the water runs so shallow that its deep

And I speak as the chief of the drummers like Namana

returning every summer to reclaim his fore father's throne

so frustrated with the representation of what we hold most close

and since Gil Scott Heron, Amiri Baraka and Maya Angelou are all dead maybe it's finally time for HipHop's
reincarnation so poets let's go
spit a rhyme and traveled back in time to Kush
and returned with nothing but my naked soul

because we are all God's and we are all nigga's
living with our eyes closed just trying to find home
hero's and shero's of the people, we are Ghetto Griot's

Blood On My Pen

Blood on my pen

Fire on my tongue

Embalming fluid in my chest

It would be best if death

Would just come

A dead poet

Only because I own it

While you was writing for life

I gave mine so you could write

"The fact that we had an entire black presidency and didn't even leave a dent in the prison practices of the greatest incarcerator on earth is a travesty and a tragedy."

-Mumia Abu-Jamal

A Crack In The Wall

If every stanza that I write

Had the power to remove

At least one brick from the wall

On which Mumia Abu-Jamal is forced to write

Maybe I would be able to deconstruct

this country's corrupt prison system

by the end of this poem
Maybe I could get more minds open than closed cells
But it's clear to see
that there is no cure to the virus of injustice
in the system
for those trapped in the justice system
without bail

But "We Want Freedom" now
Even if we have to scream it
"Live From Death Row"
Just read "The Writing On The Wall"
and it ain't hard to tell
That where still living in hell
cause from both
"The Classroom and The Cell"
pipelines fill up with more
black gold than petroleum wells
Indeed a crude system

But still through the night we fight
as "Death Blossoms"
witness the resistance and resilience
of God's children still breathing inside closed coffins
for even with
"All Things Considered"
we still carry
"The Faith Of Our Fathers"
regardless of the bars that lock us within
For you can never silence the voice of a man

who's pen screams ten times louder

than the sound of the bullets he never fired

But since

"political power grows from the barrel of a gun"

Let

"the voice of the voiceless"

Fire a thousand rounds

Or better yet five shots from downtown

as corrupt cops surround

Cause obviously standing with hands raised

is an exercise in political futility

when the target is on your memory

and they've already dug your grave

While the FOP flopped on the play

as the "prosecutor in robes" Sabo-taged the situation

Would make more sense if

I wrote letters to satan in brail

Cause those who make fortunes on incarceration

will never feel the plight

Of those who's blood stains sustain

this nations disdainful foundation

Not when the private prison system is a representation

of the American plantation reincarnated

as the western world's latest corporation

used as a subsidiary to profit off of pain

and human subjugation

And no politics or failed pardons

from corrupt officials and puppet presidents

can fix this
Not when it was evident
that the police and prosecution
worked in cohort to distort the evidence
and threaten key witnesses
before they even got the chance
to take the stand
Cause in this land
it hardly matters if you're a Free-man
you'll still get found murdered the next day
with a dope needle stuck in your vain
No difference from when
the devil moved on MOVE
by literally stomping Life
from the hands of Africa
as the police bombed a house
full of innocent black citizens
11 victims 5 of them children
as 50 blocks burned like a war torn village

So let every line I spit
represent another shattered brick
You can call it conspiracy
or simply the right to fight write and resist
I can never forget fist raised like parchments
in Philly with the panthers marching
we shut down an entire city block
while traffic stopped as horns blew in solidarity
And this system of convictions
racist bigots and capitalist business interest

is a mess

so the people remain oppressed

and equally vexed

wretched of the earth

buried beneath the turf of conquest

while the press remains pressed to compress

the woven words of the blessed

Nonetheless

They can never silence the truth

Not even under threat of death

Bullet in your chest as proof

They uncouth

Against it all persist and stand tall

The crack in the wall

That they still can't fill/feel

Mumia Abu Jamal

Editor's note:

Fuck the police

When the artist becomes activist

Just to get more people

to follow

Them on the internet

Both art and activism suffer the consequence

Of listening to yo bullshit

If this poem doesn't piss somebody off

I've failed

"Jails and prisons are designed to break human beings, to convert the population into specimens in a zoo - obedient to our keepers, but dangerous to each other."

-Angela Davis

"The Meaning Of Freedom"

There is a fine line

between activism

And those who act as activists

Those who bello loudly

in the moment

Yet maintain no momentum

in the struggles needed

In order to motivate movements

into breathing

If I am to stand upon the hill

and scream freedom as my right

Let my amplification device

Be a stick of dynamite

A thundering heard of words

Charging like a militia into the fire

There should be no moderate

to the cause of it

because you can't fight racism

and white supremacy

politely

It's not the far left where we stand
But rather on the demand
for the truth
Black rage contained in flames of frustration
disillusioned with the illusion
given through a limited political vision
and 2 party system
Where both parties propagate
the same system
that helps a corporatized nation maintain profit
off of mass incarceration
Yea they loved Bill but Bills bills
help to build those prisons

And prisons will never be obsolete
Not even a meaningful suggestion
when they serve as a core component
of capitalism by humans used as capital
to make a killing
at literally making a killing
while black women and children
are deprived
"The meaning of freedom"
is not freedom if that freedom
is only achieved through the compromise
of more black lives

If nothing else this last election
Should have finally proven to the blind

that a ballot cannot change this country
but rather only reveal it's true colors
Its far time we expose
that lady liberty actually has no clothes
and pill back the lies of the bourgeoisie
There is no democracy
Political irrelevancy
it matters not rather it was to be
Trump, Bernie or Hillary
Not when we participate
in a political system
that propagates the system of white supremacy

And you can call it leftist writing
And radicalism
prone to incite riots
race fighting unrest and division
But what you see as radical
Is merely righteous resistance
in the name of thee oppressed
Not a terrorist threat
But a promise to abolish
The prison industrial complex
Police brutality and the culture of racism
capitalism and death
Cause yes the devil is a liar in the flesh
and politicians are wicked minions for hire
And no if all lives mattered
Than we wouldn't have to say
Black lives matter to begin with

                                              Yet when they see our house in flames
                                              The response is to pour water on their own
                                                   So maybe it's time that we bring
                                                              the fire to your home

Note to white allies

I don't want you as an ally

If your assistance means assimilating us

Back into the same system

that caused the problem to begin with

Note to black conscious people

If the primary purpose of your black power

Is to punch on other black people psychologically

Than your black power fist is actually doing the work of

white supremacy

"the job of the conscious

is to make the unconscious conscious"

not beat up the unconscious for being unconscious

nobody is born with enlightenment

it's a process

we all arrived with closed eyes out of triple darkness

Note to the woke

You can't stay woke and chase the American dream

You better wake up or die nigga

But it seems that the righteous

Are now labeled as thee extreme

That's why every word that I'm writing

Is me fighting for my people to be free

SCOTT FREE

If the black woman is simply expendable

Then God must be dead

and emancipation proclamation statements disgraced in misplaced buckets of complacent hatred drenched in paper pimp smacked amendments present the perforated proof that slavery has never ended

This is not poetry but rather written realism at the expense of senseless southern strangleholds in the image of plantation chokeholds on black households extended and antebellum sentiments revisited

Auction blocking bags of cotton whips massaging black backs lashes left tracks carving confederate state maps white Christ's beneath white sheets pop-locking while God's eyes are watching fuck sexy they bringing slavery back

And oppression is a classic record that never gets finished spinning instead they just remix it every couple millenniums so to me "we shall overcome" sounds no different than
"go down Moses"

Isaac Hayes holding golden staffs composing open rough drafts cause even after adding Numbers with Deuteronomy the chill-dren of Is-real still failed to do the math

And segregations Exodus only proved that deception remains the precedent

Word to Aquil Mizan the post-civil rights error (era) was nothing less than slow death in disguise

So I guess reconstructions true post traumatic production was nothing more than the Genesis for black genocide

Sweet chariots of fire swing low on the wings of Shagefo blind folded by lies

Niggez knees need rest fuck your prayers I'm telling you the God we were given has already died

Illogical un-washable sinning committed cause our women have been crucified

Vehemently victimized subsequently entire families and communities at an irreconcilable divide

Emotional degradation through corporate media demonization aiding in the tripling of the black female prison population such shocking revelations for over 15 years of unjust incarceration for 2 Mississippi sisters in the face of false accusations consecutive double life sentences for a robbery they didn't commit in which only $11 dollars was taken no injuries sustained or weapons to claim

Restrictions of an unjust justice system founded upon un-honorable laws where judges with no honor dishonor the courts cause

"Cast Iron Roses" are decomposing behind iron bars in deplorable conditions health slipping from kidney disease and 5th state diabetic symptoms

Jamie and Gladys Scott were knocking on closed walls yet the state of Mississippi had not heeded their calls

Corrupt politicians refusing to listen even after vigorously maintaining their innocence

Another consistent vision of continuous imperialistic traditions and senselessness so Slangston refuses to relinquish these revolutionary convictions

My ink linked with the blood of Lincoln mingled with poison penmanship seconds before stabbing the statue of liberty in her neck with the tip because the bullshit the bitch spew from her lips don't mean shit

But I'm just a poet with nothing but saliva that's hardly potent enough so I persist to spit

My mother's warm breast milk in the face of Willie Lynch even though America is far from deserving of such heavenly sustenance

and this instance is just one horrific representation of countless cases of black women being denied basic human benefits

in an attempt to assassinate the Goddess

spiritual disembodied departure from her proper position

as Satan's $alesmen commences to sharecrop our souls off to the lowest bidder

it seems we be spitters following drinking gourds filled with polluted water no wonder my poetry sounds so bitter and no I am not a patriot and this is not my nation

within my ear drums translations statements such as
"yes we can" just sound like "thank you Satan"

the Scott Sisters are more than political prisoners this is beyond black liberation

Malcolm X made me

I'm just following my training

Sojourner raised me

I'm just rearranging your complacency

with pages of ancient Isis papers as proof

cause until the day every one of my follicles' turn "gray" I will remain a "witness" to the Truth

justice shall never be a possibility in a society founded on slavery so neither should be peace

"free at last" nigga free my A$$ from cheek to shining cheek until the truth can be spoken free

With limitless African genius spilling from ceilings and we don't need any beats

Set these spoken words Scott Free, set the Scott Sisters free!

and let our hearts hold no peace until the Scott Sisters are SCOTT FREE!!!!

the Scott sisters are now FREE

But how can we have free

When the city's feel like slave ships

And the classrooms feel like prisons

And the prisons feel like plantations

The coltan in our cell phones

Like cotton caught inside broken bones ready to explode

The big bang inside the galaxy of the Black American universe began in the bottom of boats
As ancestors held hands with the sacred
in the belly of slave ships
The encoded poems are ancient downloaded into our DNA
Melanin and melody made survival tactics for African masses
Downloaded into the soul matrix of the planet

Our creativity is spiritual
Gods heartbeat a drum

We dance through the pain as ritual

"Since Blacks, others of color and the oppressed are the overwhelming majority of people in prison, we need to seriously think about creating parole boards that mirror the people in prison, that is, "People Parole Boards."

-Sundiata Acoli

Nu Afrikan Mantra

There are times
when the weight of a poem
in your hands
hardly feels heavy enough
When you wish your words
could wield the heavy of a gun
The impact of a bullet
Would rather carve your words
on hollow tips
than loose leaf
and speak a full clip
rather than recite a forgotten mantra for monsters
When spells spoken won't kill the devil
we often wish for more effective ammunition
than dead diatribes of failed diction
To solicit satan for his sympathy

And they'll probably call this violent
Incendiary
An anti-American diatribe of blackness gone O.P.

And they'd be right

Cause there comes a point

where you'd rather fight than write

Where vocal turns vengeance

So war seems highly logical

And peace not a proper incentive

No longer as inventive

Preach peace and get lynched

From trees

Get locked in chains beneath boats

And forced into labor

Get locked behind bars in prisons

and forced into labor

Shot up with your hands up

Or strangled until you can't breathe

Countless peaceful black bodies

hung like ornaments in the breeze

You can preach peace every time

you touch a mic for your entire life

and still get shot dead on a balcony

in board daylight

So don't speak to me about democracy

in a country that openly

Wears it's hypocrisy like a favorite outfit

Where they've never refused to use

The constitution as a shooting range target

while firing plenty live rounds

into the illusion of liberty

a consistency of deception and non-sense

their greatest statements of justice
have routinely proved to be absolutely counterfeit
They themselves have written thousands of words
concerned with the ways of freedom
equality and benevolence such beautiful rhetoric
Than continuously use metal tools
to do the thee exact opposite

So I'm expected to use words against weapons
Remain non-threatening
While everyday death swallows life
As light turns into night
And all I'm supposed to do
is sit here and write
But what if I told you
that the only time the pen
is mightier than the sword
are on the days when the sword doesn't strike

So this poem isn't just a raised fist
But an uplifted assault rifle
held inside it
What's the point of a speech
and negotiations for peace
when police regularly choose to greet
in the language of aimed heat
You could get stopped on the New Jersey turnpike
for a so called busted head light
step out with arms raised
and still get sprayed on site

and yet they'll expect you to express regret
for defending your own life
after being locked in a cage
for the rest of your life
40 plus years and it ain't right
That they tried to bury Sundiata Acoli alive
cause when the board for patrol denies
they can determine how long the sentence
should be extended
and set their own term limits
so this isn't just another piece
but speech to be loaded into guns
I might shoot to salute and fire 21 for the panther 21
cause I refuse to choose or include to seek
in the ruse of peace
until all political prisoners are set free
and to those lost rest in peace
But how can I rest on peace and protest
from unrest
begging this nation for basic rights
as long as they have zero respect for my very life
Yet I'm just expected to use words
as my only weapon
while I sit here and write

If poetry is protest than this poem is a hand grenade wrapped in a prayer

"Prisons are big business in the United States, and the building, running, and supplying of prisons has become the fastest growing industry in the country. This super-exploitation of human beings has meant the institutionalization of a new form of slavery." -Assata Shakur

Escaped Slave

Poetry as protest
Poetry as political statement
Poetry as railing cry on paper
Poetry as unrest
Poetry as heartbeat
Poetry as life
In response to death
Insurgent art placed back
Into context
Truth with no chaser
The beautiful struggle on our breath
And when oppressed
Poetry becomes terrorist
Under threat

Or at least according to the agencies
Ridiculous list
Those who legally lynched
Assata
And would now dare label
"She who struggles" for liberation
As a terrorist

But wherever there is oppression
There will be resistance

Because from plantations to prisons
The fight to abolish the institution of slavery
has clearly not ended

Convicted in the incident they call for extradition
Under the guise of being brought to justice
via a legal system
where none actually exists
Shot while attempting to surrender
Beat and tortured while hospitalized
Found guilty in an absolute farce of a trail
by an all-white jury
than routinely abused inside prison

wait I'm sorry.

I was looking for the justice???

You can measure the history of American cruelty
evil political practices enacted
and police brutality
than watch it repeat
And find absolutely no trace of justice...

So what the fuck is this?

Nat Turners bible baptized in
the blood of a blind Potiff
no poetic production or divine passage

This is a letter written

from Oshun to Lazarus

while overwhelming oppression

and political repression

tap dances on top of Freedoms

Ashes

So let the truth rise through the masses

like Madam Shakur from the confinement of a cell

Escaping you maggots

Finally Free

"Hands Off"

Cause even Jesus was a political prisoner

so COINTELPRO couldn't stop the politicized

black militant messiah

on the rise from inside your minds fire

while black faces in high places

do the devils deeds motivated by greed

the people need those willing to do what's right

my heart beats a solemn drum

dedicated to those

who's sacrifice paved the way for liberation

so we sing for Assata a song in honor

Refugee of Gods good fight

Against the capitalist evil tendencies

of imperialism presented

through the privatized prison industry

Jail cells like hell drenched in blood and the smell of misery

for as long as most of the people

                    on planet earth are not free

            the battle for the future will never

                                        be done

                                The fight can be won

                                The fight can be won

                                The fight can be won

                                The fight must be won

But poetry hardly lives up to the needed task

Cause to be honest a lot of poets

Be str8 ass

A whole lot of fans

And social media hype

But no respect for the craft

Just throw on a beret

Than utter some hashtags

and a bunch of famous black names

now you a poet

As if you copt the pseudo conscious nigga starter kit

prior to signing the open mic list

Lyricists who's lips drip with spoken herpes

Would be better to burn every letter you write

Cause that shit aint fire

The foundation for what you stated as broken as that trophy

But forget the Kontroversy

Cause yea I get it

Nigga you couldn't get your writing up

If you held a workshop in orbit

and they like Slang we can't stand ya

Why you so mad bro

Nah

I guess we just poetry snobs

Been on the job so long

That our hands bleed stanzas

I blame my coach

Forget status and rhyme skills

Cause when Lamar Hill is literally

Showing your squad the ropes

You got no choice but to make every quote

So dope it feel like your lungs broke

Now how's that for wordplay

These words aint for play

Slam poetry this more like

Spoken MMA

Metaphors Made ARTtillery

And aint no progression for your pen game

without the pain

It seems that I been insane

ever since I fail off stage

Aint really nothing left to say

"etc etc... the body of my literature is bigger than South America"

"Most of today's black convicts have come to understand that they are the most abused victims of an unrighteous order."

-George Jackson

Black Dragon

History is a weapon
That can be used
as the ammunition for truth

Or as a barrow of lies
supplied to the blind
who choose to refute that truth
effectively carrying out the work
of the enemy in their stead
Our history is unfortunately
one filled with proof of the latter

There is no freedom for the future
without first reclaiming the past
My saliva structured into revolutionary stanzas
comprised of sacred scribes
brought alive on behalf of the "Soledad"
spoken into blasts my mouth a shotgun

I am the violent scream that can't be silenced
I am the quiet of the storm ready to explode
Lock and reload
I am Angela's sawed off inside
John Jackson's palms
The truth strapped to a time bomb

The struggle inside
A riot in our veins

A trial taken hostage
Court house under aim
"Blood In My Eye"
Prison on fire
Pen full of flames

This is a letter to God
To send more guns
A text message to heaven
Rain fire on these devils
They've long since expended
The length of your divine patience
the ancestors have been waiting
They are due
Reparations paid in blood
and refuse rebirth
Until you pay what you owe nigga

The gate is open
And the dragon cometh
Breathing black fire from the throat
Of a 9 mm heartbeat
A panther in his lungs
Blood is what we write
Assassin in site
Revolution in the yard
This ain't ink or bars
But tears spilling from a silenced pen
A buck shot from the mind
Bullet exploded in your spine

> A spirit lifted into the forever
> The dragon will never die

they say

Bmore poets rarely use trigger warnings

But what's the point when the city where you living

Is the trigger

So what you write might start to sound like

live rounds from a rifle

Less likely to go viral and more like survival

No points for trigger warnings when your throat

is a fully loaded strap

So you might sound less like SlamFind and more like SMACK

Unsure whether you got a mic or magnum cocked

So you just might write less like Rudy and more like Tay Roc

Black apologist posing as poets sound hesitant

Your team vs Slammageddon that's ants against elephants

Baltimore vs all yall whores

We spit that real life while yall still reciting metaphors

I been on that extraterrestrial alien Shamballah shit since

day one

So you already know I know what the meta is for

"The time in the hole had forced me to quiet reflection and contemplation. I resolved to never give up my struggle for freedom for me or my people. So the penitentiary represented to me just another level of struggle."

-Marshall Eddie Conway

(Baltimore Black Panther and former political prisoner)

Soldier For Liberation

The voice of truth sounds loudly
From inside of a cage
Never defined by the circumstance
But the actions committed
in the beautiful struggle against it

So In an attempt to declare
"Marshall Law" on the movement
Hoover moved in
and quite devilish
With counter measures
To try and counter our intelligence
They lied
Because you can't counter
the intelligence of a liberated mind

Targeting key points
of the black panther leadership
With frame ups of police murder
at the hands of party members
Created an epidemic against the resistance
by charging panthers with the killing of police
As false of a narrative
as the myth of blacks raping white women
in the Jim Crow south

or Emmett Till whistling

Leading to a series of legal lynchings

And to spite consistent insistence of his innocence

it took nearly 44 years

due to the the corrupt court system

to gain his freedom

in the face of a faulty conviction

see they want to gentrify your mind

with lies and propaganda

than kill off our leaders with impunity

and call us terrorists

for trying to defend

and build up our own communities

But the bars that confine

Cannot define the power

of an empowered mind

Determined to free others

For the dedication for liberation

First begins with the re-education

of the people

followed by the unification

of all who oppose slavery

In all of its forms

While they view Baltimore

through the distorted lens

of CNN and "the Wire"

yet here come the funding

after we start to light some shit on fire

While they mislabel

the language of the unheard

as mere riots

you can't silence the solace

of a righteous uprising

It is imperative

that we write our own narratives

because if you don't tell your own story

someone else will surely tell it for you

and choose to confuse the medias

agenda lead interpretation of your truth

as the truth they use

instead of "The Real News"

Dissemination of incriminating

Misinformation and instigation

created by American Terrorism

"Automatic Democratic Fascism"

So forget change

and attempts to simply rearrange

the gains of colonialism

We must deconstruct the entire system

The solution is to liberate

and build our own institutions

Continue the resistance

persistent in our will to survive

Marshall "Eddie" Conway

Free... And Alive!

Now

Look

I'm just trying to murder the MAAFAA

Turn slams into operas

Smoking dat Big Poppa mixed with Black Chakra

HipHop blended with slave hymns

Poetry you gotta bleed to complete

Call me Amiri Bars-Raka

Blood on my pen

Fire on my tongue

Embalming fluid in my chest

It would be best if death

Would just come

A dead poet

Only because I own it

While you was writing for life

I gave mine so you could write

America On Fire

"Then we can listen, without the undercurrent of desire
to first set yo ass on fire"-Amiri Baraka

When they come for me

The first thing they'll see

Will be flames

We have been burning since we got here

We have been holding fire since birth

Dying to open our hands

And let the wind speak for us

My language is burning tongue

Opened wound and blackened son

Bullets on black skin remind me

That melanin and memories are alike

Fading as night falls

We have been holding history in our lungs for so long

That death feels like breathing

Life feels like dying

I am dead man speaking

America

You are a mouth made of maggots

A crucifix carved from cold colored carcasses

warped around the sun

There must be fire

There must be burning echoes

Of liberated song laughing

Over a symphony of singing guns

We have been human in the company of savages for so long

That our hue-manity breaks like

Shattered drums

like opened bread

Body blessed of burning bible verse

Ripped to shreds

Because if devils can trust in god

Than my faith was born dead

How the fuck

Can I put air back in the room

When all they do is take our breath

We scream with corpse filled cadence

Another poem pregnant with

bloody ink and brown broken bodies

As if black rage is just anger for angers sake

When black rage is sacred

Black rage is survival

in the face of everything that has

tried to kill us and killed us

failing to keep us dead

Black rage is thee alternative

to our hands around your necks

So many names staining our fingerprints

That my palms have no room left for eulogy

An embodiment of dead bodies draped over microphones

I wrote this poem already

I wrote this poem already

I already wrote this poem

My writers block is stained in the blood of my people

So these words better burn beautiful

Better scorch the earth

they bury us beneath

My pen feels bullet heavy

Heavier than this heart

These words are torn flesh

Baptismal of black tears

on brown face as notebook

And all that I can write is a burning page

Burning death and broken spirit

Coffins caught in my capillaries

Graveyard in my chest

Heartbeat as crematory

My soul is on fire

And America you are next!

The moment we get tired of all these black poems

Is the moment we become complacent

with all this black death

This isn't a black poem

Not when the body of my text

Reads like a black body

Trying to reclaim its stolen breath

Another autopsy as literary art

I am tired of holding writing workshops in the morgue

with hashtags as prompts

I'd rather use my hands to hold guns

Than write poems

Yesterday

I tried to meditate

And all the mantras sounded like madness

Sounded like

My mouth mumbling over melanated names made martyr

made...

Amadou

Oscar

Alton

Tamir

Sandra

Trayvon

Rekia

Patrick

Philando

Eleanor

Darrien

Russell

Michael

Malissa

Darnisha

Jordan

Tarika

Jonathan

Tyrone

Shawn

Freddie

Yvette

Tanisha

Eric

Aiyana

The ancestors won't speak to me because they're too busy with orientation

How long before I have to write this same autopsy

For...

Diondre

for

Mohamed

Derick

Deniero

Kraileani

JahNeal

Mecca

Joy

Brion

Jacob

Kenneth

Alexander

Chin-Yer

Ma'issa

Maren

Nakia

Sadiyah

Devlon

Olu

Michelle

Natasha

Ramond

Aquil

Eric

Joy

Naomi

Daniel

David

Lennette

How long

before I have to write this same autopsy

for my own

before I am forced to wrap my family and friends

in a shroud made of metaphors and write their names on it

Before they have to pick up a pen and edit my body

And I will not ask your government for help

no I will not pray to your god for protection

Fuck that nigga

Oshun disapproves

Yemaya disapproves

Ogun and Obatala

demand fire and truth

Shango said

he ready to let them thangs go

It's time to take the targets off of our bodies

and put them on theirs

June Jordan's poetry haunts my day-mare's asking

"What if every time they kill a black boy we kill a cop?"

What if for every black life taken

we burn a city

We engulf a senator

in flames

Our history is a history of being baptized

in this country's love made lighter fluid

And if "I too am America"

Than we going burn together

We going light this mother fucker

On FIRE

Not because we want to watch it burn

But so that maybe they will finally see the light

About the Author

Born in and influenced by the HipHop era, yet at the same time always acknowledging the foundations laid down by fore runners and trailblazers such as Langston Hughes, Amiri Baraka, Gil Scott Heron, The Last Poets, Sonia Sanchez, Nikki Giovanni, June Jordan, Jaki Terry, Saul Williams, Jessica Care Moore, Taalam Acey, E The Poet Emcee, etc... Slangston Hughes attempts to bridge the gap between the legacy paved through the Harlem renaissance and Black Arts Movement with the innovative but yet rebellious spirit of HipHop culture. Slangston Hughes is a National Slam Champion based out of Baltimore, Maryland. He's a decorated performer winning many competitions and awards across the country. Hughes also is the Director of Youth Poetry at Dew More Baltimore and is the artistic director and lead literary instructor for Dew More Baltimore. Slangston Hughes was the first ever Word War grand slam champion in 2008 (Baltimore) and the 2010 Baltimore Crown Awards "Poet of the Year" recipient and a member of the Philly Pigeon Slam team that competed nationally at Southern Fried Poetry Slam in 2012. In 2007 Hughes released "Slanguage Arts" the album which was critically praised as "A deeply profound representation of this generation's next and most important radical poetic voice" by Umar Bin Hassan of The Last Poets. Hughes' 2012 album Ghetto Griot vol 1 (Tubman City Times) is an epic of truth that brings together HipHop and Afro Beat Rhythms with the revolutionary spirit of the black consciousness movement and ancestral spirit of the griot and Nommo (speaking words to life) tradition. His work has been published in the Poets ' America anthology via the Kratz Creative Writing Center. (2014) And in 2015 published his first collaborative literary work along with author/prosaist Devlon E. Waddell as part of E.M.B.O.D.Y. (Ethereal Manifestation By Overtly Developing You). Slangston in addition is the founder and Co-SlamMaster/curator of Speak Out: Slammageddon as well as a member of the 2016 Slammageddon Baltimore team that won the National Poetry Slam. Slangston is also the lead slam coach for the Baltimore City Youth Poetry Team (Dew More Baltimore) that won the Brave New Voices International Youth Poetry Slam in 2016.

"Street poetry, not because it is merely poetry from or for the street, but because evidently I want every word that I speak to eventually become concrete"
.-Slangston Hughes

"Slangston Hughes' work is literary astral travel; a range that begins at provocation and vectors to profound nourishment. He is Sonny Rollins sharpening his chops during an early 60's Brooklyn Bridge sabbatical or a divine reverend in a late 70's project basement rec room preaching over hip hop beats with words that uprock and windmill. Quite simply, I've been acquainted with Slangston Hughes's work for several years and his authenticity, gift and integrity make him one of my precious few favorites."
-Taalam Acey

"So many poets today. So many visceral fiery words of love penetrating the annals of our collective history...but only few willing to raise the sharpened metal of ogun, erzulie or shango—gutting out not mere effigies posing as presidents— but the vital organs and very soul of oppression and its systems and institutions. What a blessing and honor to have engaged in the mystical act of artistic creativity with Slangston Hughes!! This Black life in America shit is far from being a crystal stair yet Slangston holds his own raising one new brilliant "I don't give a fuck!" young warrior poet at a time. Passionate, furious women and men of letters. Passing on the ancient torch of verse among lonely red brick, circling armies of ravens, epitaphs on tombstones reading, "fuck you whores", chicken boxes, hot dugs, steamed crabs, and pigs that do dirt and run free. Confirming that the undying expression of love for your people is the highest and truest form of revolution. In the words and sentiment of Slangston Hughes: "Fuck you! And Fuck them too!! I am Jesus at a peaceful protest fully strapped!!!!"
-Bashi Rose

Made in the USA
San Bernardino, CA
01 May 2017